Finding the
Leader in You

Also Available from ASQ Quality Press:

Making Change Work: Practical Tools for Overcoming Human Resistance to Change
Brien Palmer

From Quality to Business Excellence: A Systems Approach to Management
Charles Cobb

The Six Sigma Path to Leadership: Observations from the Trenches
David Treichler

The Change Agent's Guide to Radical Improvement
Ken Miller

The Change Agents' Handbook: A Survival Guide for Quality Improvement Champions
David W. Hutton

Office Kaizen: Transforming Office Operations into a Strategic Competitive Advantage
William Lareau

The Recipe for Simple Business Improvement
David W. Till

The Trust Imperative: Performance Improvement Through Productive Relationships
Stephen Hacker and Marsha Willard

Transformational Leadership: Creating Organizations of Meaning
Stephen Hacker and Tammy Roberts

From Baldrige to the Bottom Line: A Road Map for Organizational Change and Improvement
David W. Hutton

The Executive Guide to Improvement and Change
G. Dennis Beecroft, Grace L. Duffy, John W. Moran

To request a complimentary catalog of ASQ Quality Press publications, call 800-248-1946, or visit our Web site at http://qualitypress.asq.org.

Finding the Leader in You

A Practical Guide to Expanding Your Leadership Skills

Anton G. Camarota

ASQ Quality Press
Milwaukee, Wisconsin

American Society for Quality, Quality Press, Milwaukee 53203
© 2004 by American Society for Quality
All rights reserved. Published 2004
Printed in the United States of America

12 11 10 09 08 07 06 05 04   5 4 3 2 1

Library of Congress Cataloging-in-Publication Data
Camarota, Anton G., 1954–
    Finding the leader in you : a practical guide to expanding your leadership skills /
    Anton G. Camarota.
        p. cm.
    Includes bibliographical references and index.
    ISBN 0-87389-630-0 (soft cover, perfect bound : alk. paper)
    1. Leadership.   2. Executive ability.   3. Executives—Training of.   I. Title.

    HD57.7.C353 2004
    658.4′092—dc22   2004008261

ISBN 0-87389-630-0

Publisher: William A. Tony
Acquisitions Editor: Annemieke Hytinen
Project Editor: Paul O'Mara
Production Administrator: Randall Benson
Special Marketing Representative: David Luth

ASQ Mission: The American Society for Quality advances individual,
organizational, and community excellence worldwide through learning, quality
improvement, and knowledge exchange.

Attention Bookstores, Wholesalers, Schools, and Corporations: ASQ Quality Press
books, videotapes, audiotapes, and software are available at quantity discounts
with bulk purchases for business, educational, or instructional use. For
information, please contact ASQ Quality Press at 800-248-1946, or write to
ASQ Quality Press, P.O. Box 3005, Milwaukee, WI 53201-3005.

To place orders or to request a free copy of the ASQ Quality Press Publications
Catalog, including ASQ membership information, call 800-248-1946. Visit our
Web site at www.asq.org or http://qualitypress.asq.org.

Quality Press
600 N. Plankinton Avenue
Milwaukee, Wisconsin 53203
Call toll free 800-248-1946
Fax 414-272-1734
www.asq.org
http://qualitypress.asq.org
http://standardsgroup.asq.org
E-mail: authors@asq.org

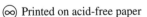 Printed on acid-free paper

For Mariko, who taught me kindness.

Contents

List of Figures, Tables, and Exercises .... *xi*

SECTION 1 THE STRUCTURE OF EXCELLENCE **1**

Chapter 1 Introduction **3**
What This Book Is About 5
The Being of Leadership 6
The Doing of Leadership 7
Your Leadership Journey 7

Chapter 2 Trouble at SpeedyCo **9**
The Budget Meeting 9

Chapter 3 Understanding Human Experience **13**
Leadership Lessons—Meeting the Invisible Guide 20
Leadership Lessons—Being and Doing 22

SECTION 2 THE BEING OF LEADERSHIP **29**

Chapter 4 Lunch at the Greenery **31**

**Chapter 5   Remembering Who You Are: Metaphors
               of Identity** **35**

Knowing What You Want 35
Leadership Lessons: Discovering Your Leadership
    Metaphor 43
Leadership Lessons: Understanding Your Leadership
    Purpose 43

Chapter 6   A Walk on the Beach **53**

Chapter 7   What Matters Most: Values and Beliefs **59**

Knowing What Is Important 59
Leadership Lessons: Articulating Your Values and
    Supporting Beliefs 63

SECTION 3   THE DOING OF LEADERSHIP **67**

Chapter 8   What Leaders Really Do **69**

Chapter 9   Dinner at La Fontaine **75**

**Chapter 10   Orientation: Identifying Well-Formed
               Outcomes** **79**

The Importance of Outcomes 79
Leadership Lessons: Defining What You Want 80

Chapter 11   An Afternoon on the Bay **85**

Chapter 12   Alignment: Resonating with Your Truth **91**

Understanding Emotional Intelligence 91
The Emotional Intelligence Process 92
Leadership Lessons: Developing Emotional Awareness 96
Leadership Lessons: Practicing Emotional
    Self-Management 102
Communicating from Needs 105
Reframing 108

Chapter 13   An Evening on the Island **113**

Chapter 14   Motivation: Energizing for Success **117**

Understanding Motivation 117
Leadership Lessons: Strengthening Your Motivation 118

Chapter 15   Sunrise at Satori **127**

Chapter 16   Soaring to Success **129**

Glossary *133*

Sources and References *135*

Index *137*

Figures, Tables, and Exercises

Figure 1.1   The tiger cub grew up believing he was a goat   4
Figure 3.1   The three components of NLP   14
Figure 3.2   How we experience the world   16
Figure 3.3   The five neurological levels of experience   18
Figure 3.4   Looking at the tiger   20
Figure 3.5   The being and doing of leadership   22
Figure 3.6   Balance being and doing   24
Exercise 3.1   Understanding being and doing   25
Exercise 3.2   Leadership effectiveness self-assessment   26
Figure 5.1   Identity.   36
Figure 5.2   How metaphor works   36
Table 5.1   Common leadership metaphors and their effects   40
Figure 5.3   The five basic role functions   45
Figure 5.4   Defining your leadership metaphor   47
Exercise 5.1   Defining your leadership metaphor   49
Exercise 5.2   Changing your leadership metaphor   50
Figure 7.1   Values as perceptual filters   60
Table 7.1   List of possible values   62
Figure 7.2   Examples of values and beliefs   64
Exercise 7.1   Defining your values and beliefs   65
Figure 8.1   The work of leaders   70
Figure 8.2   The inner work of leaders   71
Exercise 10.1   Specifying a well-formed outcome   82
Figure 12.1   Emotional intelligence process   95
Table 12.1   Expansive emotions   97
Table 12.2   Contractive emotions   98
Exercise 12.1   Keeping an emotional diary   100
Figure 12.2   Emotional diary   101

Table 12.3   List of basic human needs   106
Exercise 12.2 Communicating from needs   109
Figure 12.3   Tips for emotional self-management   110
Figure 14.1   The motivation process   118
Figure 14.2   Components of personal motivation   122
Figure 14.3   Our motivation helps us soar   123
Exercise 14.1 Assessing your motivational beliefs   124
Exercise 14.2 Generating emotional energy   126

SECTION 1

THE STRUCTURE
OF EXCELLENCE

1

Introduction

A long, long time ago, deep in the dense forest of the Himalayan foothills, there lived a fierce and proud tigress who was about to give birth. She was very hungry and spent many days hunting in search of food. One day, she came upon a herd of goats and gave chase. Gathering up all her energy, she leapt ravenously upon them and managed to kill one. But the stress of the leap forced her into labor, and she died as she gave birth to a male cub.

The goats, which had scattered, cautiously approached the dead tigress. They discovered the newborn cub, and in compassion adopted it and raised it as their own. As time passed the tiger grew up believing that he, too, was a goat. He bleated as well as he could, he smelled like a goat, and ate only grass and vegetables. In every respect he behaved like a goat. Yet within him beat the heart of a ferocious tiger.

Time passed and the tiger cub grew up alongside the goats. One day, however, another older tiger attacked the herd, killing a goat and scattering the others to the winds. The goats all ran away as soon as the old tiger attacked, but the tiger cub remained, completely unafraid, for he had never seen another tiger before.

The old tiger had been on many hunts and had never been as shocked as when he confronted the young tiger. He did not know what to make of the tiger who bleated like a goat, smelled like a goat, and acted in every other way just like a goat. Being a rather tough old tiger, he grabbed the younger one by the scruff of the neck and dragged him to the edge of a nearby pond. Setting him down, he compelled the young one to gaze at his reflection in the glassy surface.

The old tiger said, "Look at yourself in the water. That is you. And look at me. You are exactly like me. You are not a goat, but a tiger. Your food is not grass, but meat." The young tiger did not know what to make of the reflection in the water or the old tiger's words. He did not see the similarity to the old tiger. He bleated piteously and shifted his weight from paw to paw.

Figure 1.1 The tiger cub grew up believing he was a goat.

Frustrated by this lack of comprehension, the old tiger dragged the young one back to the goat he had killed. There he ripped a piece of meat from the dead goat and shoved it into the mouth of our young friend.

At first the young tiger gagged and tried to spit out the raw flesh. But the old one was determined to show him who he really was, so he made sure the cub swallowed this new food. When the young one had swallowed it all, the old tiger shoved in another piece of meat, and this time a change came over the cub.

As he chewed and tasted the second piece of raw flesh and blood, he began to eat with gusto. A fiery strength flowed through his body and an excitement caused him to quiver from nose to tail. When he had finished, he stretched and opened his mouth as if in an enormous yawn. Then, for the first time in his life, the cub let out a powerful roar. It was a roar from the depths of his being, the roar of a jungle cat awakening to who he truly was.

The old tiger said, "Now that you know you are a tiger, come, let us hunt together in the forest." With that, the two tigers walked away, disappearing into the dense underbrush together.

In this Bengali folk story we hear the young tiger's roar of awakening. It is the moment of the flash of awareness, an instant of self-discovery in which we see that we have taken on an incorrect identity or are inadequately expressing our essential being. It is as though we have been living in a dream, and we suddenly wake to discover a completely different world.

The tiger cub believes he is a goat and experiences the world as a goat. His goat-based perception of reality allows him to experience only a small fraction of his total being. We know that, as a tiger, he is capable of many more perceptions, emotions, and experiences. He limited himself to becoming a goat because that was all he thought he could be, and had no one else to tell him otherwise.

Metaphorically, we are all raised as goats, conditioned by the "herd" to think, feel, and experience the world in specific, predefined ways. Our cultures, families, and communities teach us at an early age how to interpret the world. Because this conditioning is all that we know, we naturally assume the world exists just as we perceive it to be. We are the person we think we are—this is our reality.

The roar of awakening is what is missing from most of our lives. When we are truthful to our true nature and core values, our lives are more congruent with the self we are inside. It is possible that a shift in awareness is all that is needed—an old tiger taking us by the scruff of our necks and dragging us to see our true reflection in a pool.

We may catch a glimmer of our true nature as a result of dramatic and important life events—birth of a child, marriage, completing college, or the death of a family member. Or we may glide through life never sensing that we are more than we give ourselves credit for, that we could achieve far more than we allow ourselves to achieve.

The key to effective leadership is to discover the tiger within. It is casting off the "goat" conditioning to reveal your glorious and powerful inner self. It is defining who you are differently so you experience life differently. It is listening to and honoring your awakened self and leading from this connected perspective. It is being in integrity with yourself and naturally building the trust and respect of your followers.

In this book you will be guided to find your inner tiger, to become the leader that you know you can become. You will connect with yourself and see the world in a new way, and you will redefine your reality so you can become a more effective leader.

WHAT THIS BOOK IS ABOUT

This book is about what it takes to be an effective leader in today's rapidly changing world of business. It is written for you—a skilled professional in a leadership position desiring to expand your leadership skills. Whether you are a team leader, supervisor, manager, director, or executive, this book gives you a comprehensive program that shows you how to further develop your leadership skills and knowledge.

This book, much like Neapolitan ice cream, contains three parts. The first part is the story of Michelle, a manager struggling with the responsibilities of leading a company initiative. The second part explains the concepts and ideas structuring Michelle's leadership experience. Finally, the third part enables you to apply these concepts through a series of exercises that expand your leadership skills.

A central purpose of this book is to foster self-knowledge and to help you become aware of who you are as a person. Self-awareness is the underpinning for any successful leader, and this book presents a specific framework for understanding yourself that has been proved to be effective in hundreds of thousands of people worldwide. The book's focus is on your inner leader—on your finding your personal wellspring of leadership power.

Setting this book apart from other leadership books is the specific guidance provided in the self-application exercises. Together with a complete description of the self-knowledge required to be a great leader, it is a complete program designed for you, the reader, to use to gain the awareness, comprehension, and skills needed to succeed. You are guided through a series of exercises that yield both understanding and capabilities for extraordinary leadership. By following Michelle on her journey, you will enter your inner world of leadership, discovering who you are, how you see the world, and how you can best achieve your leadership goals!

These self-application exercises have been tested on thousands of people from all walks of life. They were developed using the latest Neuro-Linguistic Programming (NLP) technologies and are assembled here for the first time. Comprising a comprehensive skill set, they build on and reinforce one another, enabling you to progressively deepen your skills and understanding. They have also been updated, enhanced, and customized to meet the needs of today's leaders.

The Being of Leadership

The foundation for all successful leaders is awareness—awareness of who they are as people, awareness of what type of organizations they lead, and awareness of who their followers are. Personal awareness is based on operating metaphors, values, and beliefs, all of which determine both how one interacts with the world and what gives one's life meaning. Rather than taking an action-oriented viewpoint, this section of the book focuses the reader on understandings that color both the leader's life and the specific context in which he or she is called upon to lead.

We ask you to know who you are, what you want to be doing, and where you are going—cornerstones of effective leadership. Self-knowledge also enables you to know what is most important, as well as what is true for you. With this awareness in hand, you can act with authenticity and integrity, the foundations of leadership success. Realizing that each of us carries an individual map of reality enables any leader to address both personal and follower concerns at a deep level through metaphor and story.

The Doing of Leadership

Once you have discovered who you are as a leader and how you see the world, you will develop a set of capabilities to express yourself effectively in your leadership role. You are guided through the three basic tasks of inner leadership—setting direction, managing your emotions, and motivating your actions. You are shown a core set of leadership skills that can be developed, to varying degrees, regardless of your existing identity, beliefs and leadership context. This book guides you through a set of exercises that identify areas where your skills may be lacking and provides you with a set of foundational capabilities for inner leadership. You are also pointed in the direction of further resources for more advanced skill development.

YOUR LEADERSHIP JOURNEY

As you follow along with Michelle, you will embark on your own leadership journey. Because each step is important, all of the concepts presented will be explained and demonstrated for your complete understanding. Then you are encouraged to try the ideas on, making them your own in your own way.

You are set to embark on an odyssey of self-discovery. I invite you now to accept the call and begin your personal journey, where you will travel to exciting inner shores. You will see and experience many new ideas, and you may feel strong emotions. You will come to see yourself as a leader in an entirely new way as you pursue your own path of integrity, trust, and wholeness. Finally, through realizing what's most important, you will arrive at a place of inner stillness. From that place, you will claim your personal power as an extraordinary leader.

Let the voyage begin!

2

Trouble at SpeedyCo

THE BUDGET MEETING

Michelle, the SpeedyCo director of quality, walked down the hall to her office feeling angry and confused. This was the third time she had met with the CEO and the executive vice president of sales, and each time it had gone poorly. This meeting she had tried to get her new customer service training budget approved, only to have it pushed back amid thinly disguised looks of contempt.

At the beginning of their meeting, Tom, the CEO, had asked her why this training was so important. Michelle had replied that company success depended upon training everyone as to how customer service affected their jobs, what their customer-related job responsibilities were, and what the corporate policy further stated. Tom had replied that this new customer service initiative had become a burden and that Michelle needed to figure out a faster and easier way to accomplish the training. He made it clear that if she couldn't get it done quickly, he would have to find someone who could.

Steve, the executive VP of sales, had also chimed in. "We need to get out there in the marketplace fast and stay ahead of the competition. We can't afford to slow down for anything—they're nipping at our heels! We are ahead now and we need to stay ahead of the other players. We're right on the edge of a big win and we can't allow anything to keep us out of the game."

Michelle entered her office and glumly glanced at her plants, photographs of the company softball team and her family, and her framed diplomas. The soft glow of her desk lamp illuminated a green and blue ceramic paperweight given to her by her niece. A piece from her niece's fine arts graduation show, it had meant a lot to Michelle when she received it. Now its meaning seemed to recede into the distance as the conflict with Tom loomed large.

Michelle felt utterly discouraged and frustrated. While she had been working on this customer service initiative for months at SpeedyCo, it seemed like Tom rebuffed her at every turn. This latest budget issue seemed to be just one of many obstacles blocking her path to customer service implementation. She recalled the many late nights working with each of the project teams, defining processes, and putting their procedures in place. Now it seemed as if she had wasted her time, as if the struggle might indeed prove too much for her.

The phone rang. She answered in a downcast voice, "Hello, this is Michelle."

A familiar and friendly voice resounded from the other end. "Hi, Michelle." It was Eric, her friend from Floriant, a local manufacturing firm specializing in greenhouses and sun rooms. Eric was Floriant's vice president of human resources. He always seemed to show up just in time to help her cope with difficulties in her life.

When Michelle had had trouble with her oldest son, it was Eric who suggested that she send him to teen leadership training in Nevada. He had come back a changed boy; Michelle barely recognized him as the troubled teen she had sent away merely a month before. It seemed as if Michelle could always count on Eric to help her find solutions to her problems.

Eric and Michelle had been friends since their college days at the University of Hawaii on Oahu. Michelle often thought of their weekends surfing at Waikiki Beach and along the north shore. They had remained friends throughout the years, even after Michelle moved away, married Randy, and raised her family. Michelle had earned a bachelor's degree in international business with top honors, and Eric had stayed in Hawaii and gone on with his education, receiving a Ph.D. in psychology. Although he had never married, Eric currently had a "serious" girlfriend named Alexandra, an actress who traveled extensively making movies on location.

"How are you doing, Michelle?"

"I don't feel that great. I just finished another rough meeting with Tom and Steve. I just don't understand them and what they want. They keep talking about winning the race with speed and fast time to market, yet they also seem committed to this customer service initiative. Every time we meet it seems as if all of us end up frustrated and angry, even though we want the same things for the company."

"Do you have time for lunch today?"

Michelle replied with relief, "That sounds wonderful. I really need a break after this last meeting. Can we go to the Greenery?"

The Greenery, a restaurant featuring healthful foods made daily using family recipes, was a place in which Michelle felt very comfortable. She often took her friends to lunch there, always ordering the Seafood Salad Special. She especially liked the chocolate chip ice cream, which the waiter said was made from the owner's grandmother's favorite recipe.

"I'll pick you up in 10 minutes."

Michelle glanced at the clock and saw that it was, indeed, 10 minutes before noon. "Okay, Eric, I'll meet you by the main entrance. See you then."

After organizing a few papers on her desk, including the budget and plan for the customer service training, Michelle scanned her e-mails and reviewed the most urgent. She noted one from the human resources director announcing a fitness club opening next door and providing company-sponsored memberships. Saying she thought this was a great way to improve employee health, Michelle replied that she was interested in a membership.

Michelle left her office and walked down to the main lobby. She looked casually at the case above and left of the receptionist's desk, noting a new award there. A company-sponsored high school swim team had won the state championships. She glanced at photographs of other sports teams that SpeedyCo had sponsored. These included the softball team on which she had played third base. Michelle sighed and recalled that Tom had ordered this "Wall of Fame" installed when he was hired as CEO a year ago.

Despite her positive recollections, Michelle was having a tough time shaking feelings of aggravation and worry. It seemed to her that SpeedyCo employees raced around during the day, yet frequently they had to do things over because of mistakes. She was having a difficult time convincing Tom and Steve that taking the time to do things right in the first place is better and more cost-effective. Except for the fact that SpeedyCo's largest customer, Reliable Systems, had complained about customer service, Michelle doubted that SpeedyCo would have done anything at all. Leading the process implementations had so far proved to be a slow and painful experience.

The sound of a car horn broke Michelle's thoughts. She looked around and saw Eric waving at her from the parking lot. As Michelle walked through the lobby doors, she found herself thinking that maybe Eric could help with her dilemma. She would ask for his advice over lunch.

3

Understanding Human Experience

Each of us experiences the world in different ways. We are not always in agreement with one another, and our differing experiences of the world are frequently the cause of conflict. So how is it possible to understand how each of us experiences reality?

We live in a world of information. Our friends, family, neighbors, fellow employees, and managers are sources of "input" that we receive regularly. When you consider television, radio, the Internet, billboards, newspapers, and magazines, the average person living in the modern world is overwhelmed with information. Each of us is exposed to thousands and thousands of advertisements, messages, and bits of just plain noise as part of daily life. How do we manage this onslaught of information?

Neuro-Linguistic Programming, or NLP, explains how we experience reality and manage this information to make sense of our lives. NLP, developed by Richard Bandler and John Grinder in 1976, began as a behavioral model of how we communicate to ourselves and others. This model explains, among other things, how we process the information that comes into us from the outside world. According to Robert Dilts, NLP is defined as the study of subjective experience, and it focuses on the interaction between the human nervous system, language usage, and the body. This interaction is responsible for producing human behavior, which in turn produces both effective and ineffective results in our lives.

The "neuro" component of NLP centers on the human nervous system and how its patterns and principles shape our reality. Most if not all human cognitive processes—thinking, remembering, creating, visioning—are seen as the end results of "programs" running within our nervous system. The sum total of our subjective experience is a result of how we "process" or synthesize external information that is passed through our nervous system. Our five senses—sight (visual), smell (olfactory), hearing (auditory), taste (gustatory), and touch (kinesthetic)—make up the five "modalities" or means of representing an experience.

The linguistic component of NLP is shown to be both a product and a shaper of the human nervous system. Language is seen in its most essential function, as a binder of our experience to time and space. Effective communication is the focus here, and language use in NLP centers on how to use language to instruct, to define concepts, and to transmit ideas and feelings to others.

The third NLP component, programming, refers to the processes of human memory, learning, and creativity. These processes are viewed as programs that "run" in order to accomplish certain outcomes. The key here is to understand that NLP shows us interacting with our world through our inner programming. Our situational responses are in accordance with the type and nature of mental programs we have defined for ourselves. Certain types of programs are more effective at accomplishing certain kinds of goals than others, and an effective way to change our outcomes is to change the program we use to obtain them. These three components of NLP are shown graphically in Figure 3.1.

NLP is at its heart a modeling technology, that is, a study of human excellence and the specific behaviors and cognitive maps that compose exceptional performance. NLP creates excellence by first finding out how the brain (neuro) is operating by analyzing language patterns (linguistic) and nonverbal communications. The results of this analysis are then translated into a series of step-by-step processes (programs) that enable the skills for achieving excellence to be transferred to people in different times and

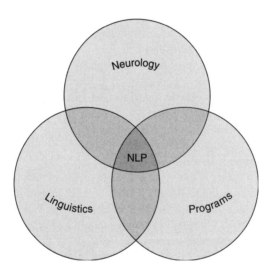

Figure 3.1   The three components of NLP.

places. The results are practical methods for achieving excellence that most people understand readily and intuitively.

NLP presupposes that people are mapmakers and that each of us makes a map of reality. NLP also presupposes that "the map is not the territory"—that our internal representations about outside events do not necessarily reflect the reality or truth of the event itself. In fact, we are prevented from knowing the truth of external events due to the deletion, distortion, and generalizations imposed on our inner world by our maps.

Typically, when something takes place in the external world, we filter that event through our internal maps. We make an internal representation that determines what we believe to be true about that event. The internal representation combines with our physiology and creates an internal emotional "state"—a happy state, a sad state, or a motivated state. Our internal representation includes pictures, sounds, dialogue, and feelings (for example, whether we feel challenged, pleased, or excited). A given emotional state is the result of the combination of an internal representation and a physiology.

According to Immanuel Kant, the process of thinking proceeds according to four basic steps:

1. I see a tiger.

2. I think I'm in danger.

3. I feel afraid.

4. I run.

The importance of this process is in understanding where our emotions and behaviors come from. Statements 3 and 4 derive from statement 2, not from statement 1, as most people assume. The way you feel and the behaviors you exhibit do not come from your environment or from the things that are happening to you or even from your direct perceptions of what is going on. It is all based on your thinking: what you choose to think determines how you feel and what you will do next. Specific thoughts create and control feelings and actions.

Let us use the example of the tiger. Just seeing a tiger does not make us afraid and cause us to run. The tiger may be in a cage or part of a circus. Our first thought may not yield the optimal feeling and action. We need to be responsible and aware of how we think about our perceptions of the world. It is a matter of defining the limits of our control: we can't control life, but we can control how we think about life and what we do in our world. By controlling our thinking, or internal representations, we are better able to manage our emotions and our actions. This thinking process is shown graphically in Figure 3.2.

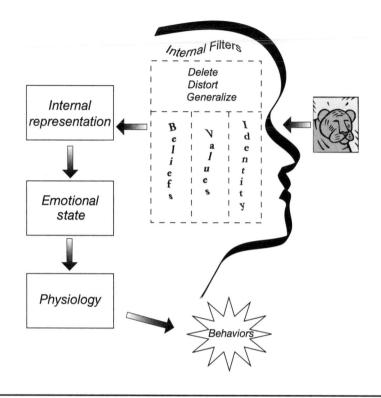

Figure 3.2   How we experience the world.

We relate to the world through our sensory input channels—visual, auditory, kinesthetic, olfactory, and gustatory (our five senses). An external event comes in through our sensory input channels and is filtered—we process the event through our map. As we process the event, we delete, distort, and generalize the information according to a number of elements that filter our perception.

We delete information when we selectively pay attention to certain aspects of our experience, overlooking, or omitting other aspects. Without deletion, we are faced with an information overload, too much for us to handle with our conscious mind. If we didn't actively delete information as part of our everyday experience, we'd end up with much too much information. In fact, you may have even heard that psychologists say that if we were contemporaneously aware of all of the sensory information coming in, we'd go crazy. That's why we delete some information—to maintain our sanity!

We distort information when we misrepresent reality and shift our experience of sensory information. There is a well-known story of distortion. A man walking along the road sees in the distance what he believes to be a snake and yells, "Snake!" However, after getting closer, he is relieved to discover that it is only a piece of rope. I'm sure you have experienced similar events, where what you thought was one thing actually turned out, after more careful examination, to be something totally different.

Distortion also helps us motivate ourselves. The process of motivation begins when we distort information by passing it through our map. We match the material to our identity, beliefs, or values and determine how to take a certain action that will reinforce one or more of them. Since a primary component of motivation is our desire to live out our identity, beliefs, and values in the world, we become motivated to act based on our distorted perception of reality.

When we generalize, we draw global conclusions based on only one or two experiences. At its best, generalization is one of the ways that we learn, by taking the information we have and inducing broad conclusions about the meaning of external events.

When two people observe the same event, why don't they have the same internal representation and subsequent response? The answer is that we delete, distort, and generalize information from the outside in different ways. Our sensory input channels, which have the same function for everyone (as shown in Figure 3.2), contain different content based on each person's life experiences, cultural and family conditioning, and unique personality. Each of us deletes, distorts, and generalizes information in different ways.

We also delete, distort, and generalize the information that comes in from our senses based on one or more of five neurological levels of experience. These awareness levels are how we become directly and personally aware of reality; when we place content in them, they become our maps of reality. The levels are Identity, Beliefs/Values, Capabilities, Behaviors, and Environment. The two "lowest" levels of experience, Behaviors and Environment, support our more abstract mental maps and enable us to interact directly with the world. Thus the content of our maps determines how we experience the world and how we react to external events.

Each of these perceptual levels determines our internal representation of any event occurring right now. Our internal representation puts us in a certain state, creates a certain physiology, and determines our behavior. The levels, included in an overall model called neurological levels of experience, are shown in Figure 3.3.

At the bottom, or most basic level, is the Environment. The Environment level involves the external conditions in which we live, and how our physical body (visual, auditory, kinesthetic, olfactory, and gustatory) senses the world. You may think of this as depending on the accuracy and precision of our "sensors" of the world, as it defines the "where and when" of our experience. Your ability to sense the external environment involves a particular part of your nervous system, how well it functions, and its ability to sense a stimulus above certain thresholds.

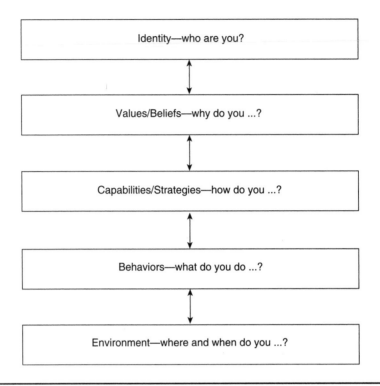

Figure 3.3   The five neurological levels of experience.

The second level, Behavior, is your ability to sense and coordinate your own body's behavior. This level determines the degree and quality of your physical actions in various situations as you move through your environment. When you access this level of experience, you are mobilizing a part of your nervous system that is deeper than your sense organs. This is the level of "what" you are doing in the world—the specific activities that you perform in the environment.

The Behavior level is also the level of state—what emotional state you bring to yourself and others. Your behavior has two basic components—how you physically move and how you feel emotionally. As we will see in Chapter 12, the keys for leadership success are understanding where emotions come from and developing a full range of emotional awareness in yourself and toward others.

The third level, Capabilities and Strategies, guides and provides direction for behaviors through a belief, strategy, or identity. At this level we encounter the first abstract component of your mental map. This level of experience has to do with your mental and intellectual capabilities—your thinking processes. It is related to "doing" in many environments. At the level of Capability you are able to select, alter, and adapt a series of behaviors to a wider set of external environments. At this level of your filter, you are perceiving and directing your actions—controlling how you perceive the world to be and directing your subsequent actions according to a specific strategy.

It is at the Capabilities and Strategies level where we find that learning new skills can change the rest of your map. Developing a new skill gives you a novel approach to understanding a subject or a situation, and it changes the "how" of your subsequent actions. For example, learning to ski changes how you behave (you can now ski down a mountain!) and changes how you experience the environment (you are now outside in the snow and cold while exercising). It may also change your belief about yourself (I am capable of surviving risky physical activity) as well as your identity (I am a skier).

The fourth level, Values and Beliefs, is where we encourage, inhibit, or generalize a particular way of thinking. Your beliefs and values transcend any particular thought, capability, behavior, or environment. At this level you are concerned with why you think what you think and do what you do, and it is here that you determine what's most important to you. Values such as family, happiness, contribution, and respect determine what capabilities we practice and what strategies we enact, what behaviors we exhibit, and how we experience our environment. Values and beliefs provide the reinforcement, motivation, and permission that either support or deny your capabilities and behaviors.

The fifth level, Identity, is the most abstract and yet the most influential. At this level you determine your overall purpose and shape your beliefs and values through your sense of self. Identity consolidates your matrix of values and beliefs into a meaningful sense of self, one that can be expressed through a metaphor, such as "Life is a game and I am a player." It is at this level where you determine who you are in your world, and then from this position you align your values, beliefs, capabilities, and behaviors to reinforce that sense of self with sensory experiences in a multitude of environments.

For example, we can use mathematics to represent the levels. Let us say the first level, Environment, is the acceleration of a car moving across a distance. The second level would represent the instantaneous speed of a car moving across the distance in terms of an hour. When we add in a number of hours for the car movement across the distance, we can then see that the third level would be the total distance traveled by the car in a given time period, or the integral of instantaneous speeds over a given time period. The fourth level could be the sum of the distances of a number of different journeys taken at different times, and so on. What this example shows is that the mathematical concept of calculus derivatives and integrals also metaphorically describes the relationship between the neurological levels.

There is another important quality of the neurological levels that is qualitatively different from a strictly mathematical representation, though. The neurological levels represent a natural hierarchy of experience, with each level controlling and organizing the information on the level below it. Changing something on an upper level changes things on lower levels; however, changing something on a lower level doesn't necessarily change things on higher levels, although it can. The primary direction of influence is from top to bottom. Each higher level controls the level beneath it, such that changes at one level will affect all the levels beneath that one. The effects of changes at a lower level on those levels above it are lessened by the very nature of the higher levels themselves.

LEADERSHIP LESSONS—MEETING THE INVISIBLE GUIDE

The neurological levels model can be deceiving in its simplicity, and most likely it is not what you think it is. It can be most clearly characterized as a two-way lens, or a stained-glass window, through which you view the world and through which your actions in the world are guided. Your perceptual filters are the vibrant infrastructure that informs your life, whether or not you are aware of it. Consciously and unconsciously, you live by your map of reality.

As shown in Figure 3.4, we see the tiger through our mental map. Our map colors and distorts reality, so it becomes difficult to sort actual conditions from the projection of our inner maps. It is important to remember that

Figure 3.4   Looking at the tiger.

our experience of the world is always colored by our map, so that we take responsibility for controlling our thoughts and managing our feelings and behaviors.

Mental maps structure our awareness and point us in the direction that becomes our path. If we are not acquainted with the content of our maps we are carried by them unconsciously, with the result that we confuse what exists objectively in the world with the image of the world supplied to us through our own distorted lens. Based on an unconscious mental map, we tend to see only one correct path, when in reality there are many paths available.

Mental maps form one of the key presuppositions around which Neuro-Linguistic Programming has formed itself—namely, that people respond to their maps of reality, not to reality itself. This statement has profound implications for leaders. We can surmise that all leadership activity, no matter how carefully thought out, is subjectively based and does not reflect the objective reality of the world. It also implies that leadership maps, as much as possible, need to be updated to reflect the organizational realities around which the leadership activities take place.

Why is it so important to become aware of your map of reality? First, your map creates your internal emotional state. Your internal emotional state then provides the charge, or impetus, for you to take action in the world. However, you also project out onto the world what you believe to be true based on your map, so you enter into a sort of self-reinforcing cycle of events. You believe something is true, see it in the world, and then act as if it were true, all the while not noticing that the truth may be something else very different indeed. This can be dangerous and undermine your credibility as a leader, for in entering into this self-reinforcing cycle you shut out the possibility of other people's truths, about which they feel just as passionately as you do. You become wrapped up in a world completely of your own devising, which most likely does not reflect the reality of your organization. Your tendency is to see the world as you are, not as it actually is.

The key tasks of inner leadership are to become aware of your map, determine if it is giving you what you want, and update it to reflect both your innermost desires and the latest technological thinking. To lead consciously, then, means becoming aware of both the content and structure of your map, its origins and nature, and taking full personal responsibility for making sure it yields your desired results in your organization. You also have the responsibility for observing your effect on others due to your map and for allowing their truths to be integrated into your perceptual filters.

These tasks are more easily said than done. For, you see, our perceptual filters exist mostly at an unconscious level! As leaders, we must look into our unconscious and bring forth what is there, examining it for relevancy and effectiveness at giving us what we truly want. The exercises in this book offer several methods for allowing you to examine your filters and deciding if you like what is there, and they offer several suggestions for possible changes.

LEADERSHIP LESSONS—BEING AND DOING

The Neurological Levels model can be applied to leadership in a different way, viewing it as an operating system for our lives. We find that the system has two parts—a being part and a doing part, as shown in Figure 3.5. These parts are very important! For not only does leadership consist of a set of capabilities and skills, it consists as well of a deep understanding of who you are as a leader, what your core identity is, and what values and beliefs you hold dear.

You act to reinforce your being—your metaphor of identity and your values and beliefs. Your doing, then, is a product of your being. It follows that, for you to perform effectively as a leader, you need to be aware of all aspects of your being—your metaphor of identity, your role and purpose, and your values and beliefs. From this place of knowing, you can act with integrity and alignment in the world.

From a leadership perspective, it's also important to note that not only do you act to reinforce your being, so do all your followers! Everyone perceives reality and takes action in the world according to their identities,

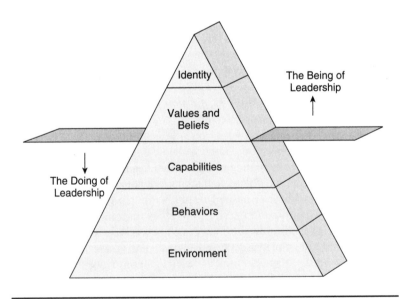

Figure 3.5   The being and doing of leadership.

beliefs, and values. The question becomes this: How do you, as a leader, maintain the loyalty and develop the enthusiasm of your followers? The answer, in a nutshell, is to provide situations in which they can actualize their identities and fulfill their beliefs and values.

To understand being more fully, think of yourself as a piece of blue glass. A piece of glass appears to be blue when light shines through because it absorbs all of the other colors of the rainbow and does not let them pass. We call the glass blue because it does not retain the blue light, but lets it pass through. Thus the glass is named not for what it possesses but for what it gives out.

Being can thus be thought of as a kind of resonance, depicting the essential qualities that you, as a leader, uniquely give out to the world. Your identity, beliefs, and values exist independently of time, and they are ways through which you make sense of and bring order to what otherwise would be chaos. Your actions in the world are always purposeful, and they spring from the well of your mostly unconscious perceptual map of reality. Thus our maps become the prime determinants of our being, the drivers of our actions in many contexts.

There is also another quality of being—projection or outpicturing—the imprinting of your identity, beliefs, and values on the world. Leadership outpicturing effectively imprints a leader's metaphor onto the organization he or she is leading, and the organization in turn develops a response known as "organizational culture." The key to understanding organizational culture, then, is to understand the leadership metaphors of those in charge and how these metaphors play out in the specific business context. The qualities of your being affect everyone who follows your lead.

Another aspect of leadership outpicturing is the assignment of roles. Everyone, according to your operating metaphor, is assigned a role and is expected to perform according to the strictures of that role. The problem is that everyone else is also living out their metaphors and assigning other people roles. The general solution? To align everyone's metaphors and their roles within their metaphors to fit with the overall organizational mission and culture. We will address this solution in detail in the chapter on identity.

Doing, in contrast to being, consists of your activities both inside yourself and in the world. It may be thought of by using the analogy of building a house. First you plan—you have an architect prepare your house drawings. Next, you select subcontractors, select a site, and begin construction. You monitor construction to make sure it goes according to plan and then test for completion by using a housing inspector. You follow a strategy (capability), which dictates certain actions (behaviors), which in turn determine the senses (environment) that you use for testing the implementation, effectiveness, and completion of the strategy.

They key to leadership excellence is to balance the being and doing, as shown in Figure 3.6. This balance requires knowing the core factors that

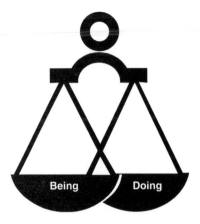

Figure 3.6   Balance being and doing.

influence how you approach your leadership tasks. It presupposes that who you are is just as important as what you achieve—in fact, who you are colors what you achieve in many ways. Leadership excellence requires that you show up authentically for your followers, and exhibit integrity and congruency in all that you do.

This book follows the two basic divisions of leadership—being and doing. The first part is dedicated to who you are as a leader and what values and beliefs are central to your existence. The second part is concerned with how you actively participate in your inner and outer worlds. This is where we introduce the three basic leadership tasks and take you through the capabilities and behaviors necessary for you to perform these tasks effectively. Throughout you will find exercises to help you integrate the concepts with your present understandings and learn the material at a deeper level. Exercise 3.1 allows you to explore the concepts of leadership being and doing a bit further so that you can gain a concrete understanding of the context of this book. Exercise 3.2 establishes a baseline against which your leadership development can be measured. It is also designed to help you understand where you may need to expand your leadership skills and how you can most effectively use the program presented in this book. Together, both of these exercises define the destination of your leadership journey—where you will develop and apply your skills.

1. How do you explain the difference between the being of leadership and the doing of leadership? _____

_____

_____

_____

_____

_____

_____

2. How are the being and doing of leadership related? How does one influence the other? _____

_____

_____

_____

_____

3. What happens when you are "doing" leadership without understanding your "being"? What are the implications of this for your organization? What are the implications of this for your personal effectiveness?

_____

_____

_____

_____

_____

Exercise 3.1   Understanding being and doing.

As a self-assessment of your leadership effectiveness, answer the questions below honestly and completely. By looking at how you perform each task and your results, you will understand where you need to improve and apply your leadership skills.

1. What are your organizational values and ethical criteria? Where are they documented? _____

_____

_____

_____

_____

2. How do you communicate organizational values and ethical criteria to employees, suppliers, and partners? How do you ensure two-way communication on these topics? How do you ascertain whether these values and criteria are understood and followed? _____

_____

_____

_____

_____

_____

3. What are your short-term and long-term organizational directions? Where are they documented? _____

_____

_____

_____

_____

_____

4. How do you communicate short- and longer-term organizational directions? How do you ensure that these directions are uniformly understood and followed by all employees? How do you ensure two-way communication on this topic?_____

_____

_____

_____

(continued)

Exercise 3.2   Leadership effectiveness self-assessment.

(continued)

5. What are your personal and organizational performance expectations? Where are they documented? _____

_____

_____

_____

_____

6. How do you communicate performance expectations? How do you hold yourself and others accountable for achieving them? _____

_____

_____

_____

_____

_____

7. How do you focus on creating and balancing value for customers and other stakeholders in your performance expectations? _____

_____

_____

_____

_____

8. How do you motivate employees and create an environment for learning, innovation, and organizational agility? How do you ensure two-way communication on these topics? _____

_____

_____

_____

_____

_____

Exercise 3.2   Leadership effectiveness self-assessment.

SECTION 2

THE BEING
OF LEADERSHIP

4

Lunch at the Greenery

Michelle and Eric were shown to a booth in the far side of the Greenery. The hostess, who recognized Michelle from her many previous visits, understood that Michelle preferred the quieter side of the restaurant, where she could talk with her companions in private.

As Eric and Michelle slid into the booth, Michelle noticed the wall across from them held some new photographs. As they settled in, the waitress, Beatrice, came over and asked them what they wanted to drink.

Michelle said, "I'll have an iced tea with lemon."

"The same for me. Thanks, Beatrice."

After Beatrice wrote down their order, Michelle asked, "Are those photographs new? I eat lunch here a lot and I haven't noticed them before."

"The owner found a bunch of old photographs of his family in the attic last month as he was cleaning out his house," Beatrice said. "They are pictures of his grandmother and grandfather right after they arrived in America. They had no money, didn't speak the language, and didn't know where they were headed. Somehow they made a successful life for themselves, raised five children, and even purchased a 200-acre ranch. Pretty amazing, huh?"

The pair nodded in agreement as Beatrice walked off to fill their drink order. Michelle thought about the obstacles that those people in the photograph must have faced, and her own situation paled in comparison.

Eric began, "So what is going on over there at SpeedyCo? It sounds like you are having a tough time of it."

Michelle flushed and said, "It just seems like no matter what I do, Tom doesn't see the need for it. Although he originally was the one who approved implementing the customer service program, he has pushed back on every one of my initiatives. Now we are going back and forth over the training budget and plan, and it seems like he just doesn't get it. Maybe you can help me figure this out. "

"What is it that Tom doesn't get?"

"It just seems as if Tom is more concerned about winning than in grow-ing his people. Although he seems to like to play by the rules, he just doesn't care about taking care of the people that work for him. He tells me that I'm slowing down the company with all of my procedures and rules."

"Michelle, have you ever thought that Tom may look at SpeedyCo in a different way from you? Didn't you tell me that he used to be a professional hockey player before he retired and went into business?"

"Yes, Eric, he was. And what do you mean by a different way of look-ing at the company? How can I understand what is going on with him?"

Beatrice walked up with their drinks and smiled broadly. "So what will lunch be today?"

Eric shifted his weight and replied, "I'll have the Inferno Chili and I think Michelle will have the Seafood Salad Special. Is that right, Michelle?" He glanced at Michelle with a twinkle in his eye.

Michelle laughed and said, "Yes, that's right!"

Beatrice wrote down their orders. Turning to Eric, she smiled and said, "I'll get those right away."

As Beatrice rounded the corner, Michelle said, "So can we get back to Tom and SpeedyCo? What do you think is going on?"

Eric paused for a few seconds, sighed heavily, and collected his thoughts.

"Michelle, Tom was and will most likely always be an athlete. He sees the world through an athlete's eyes. And what is it that hockey players do? They play games. They win competitions. Michelle, Tom sees business as a game, maybe a game of hockey. To him, SpeedyCo is all about playing the game, and what is most important is winning. Preparation is fine, but noth-ing should get in the way or slow you down when you are right in the mid-dle of a game. He wants everyone out there on the ice pulling as hard as possible for the team."

"Tom is viewing SpeedyCo from a metaphorical point of view. He is looking through the lens of his identity, seeing the business and everyone in it as playing a hockey game. This is why everyone seems to be running around frantically all the time, and why there's always time to do it over but not enough time to do it right in the first place."

Michelle gasped and said, "I see what you mean! All the time I was thinking SpeedyCo was about developing people and systems, Tom was concerned about winning the game. No wonder he seemed so put off every time I asked him to do things that would slow down the company in the short run, but would build its integrity in the long run. He was focused on winning the game at hand!"

Eric said, "That's right. And it's even a bit of a rough game, so a little 'rough stuff' from time to time is probably okay with him. So tell me, what's important to you about your job at SpeedyCo? Why did you take it?"

"I remember when I first started and interviewed with Tom. He told me he wanted me to lead their management systems project in order to beat the competition and lock in Reliable Systems as a prime customer. I remember focusing in on the training and development aspect of the project as he told me about "team" spirit. I guess what was really important was that I would get to play an important part in the growth of SpeedyCo and help to protect it and enable the team to survive and thrive."

Eric mused about that then said, "Very interesting. So what is business in general like for you?"

"Business is like parenting. I mean, I think it's important to be a guardian and caretaker of the company management systems. I'm usually willing to take full responsibility for developing and implementing any management system project, and I put the concerns of the project first."

"So for you, business is parenting, while for Tom business is a hockey game. Can you see where these two views can cause some conflict?"

"Yes, yes!" exclaimed Michelle. "My approach hasn't fit at all with what Tom is trying to achieve in the company. He's been playing a game and I've been growing a family. While he has appreciated my delineation of the rules, he also has seen all the effort that has gone into developing and main-taining the documented procedures as slowing down the players and pre-venting us from winning the game. So how can I shift things and be successful at this project?"

"I think it is a matter of aligning your metaphors, or perhaps nesting them. Maybe you could look at the situation as growing a family that is ded-icated to playing the game? Being a parent and guardian of the players? Or even have Tom see you as one of the team coaches?"

Michelle said, "I think that's great! I'm going to change my approach to the project. I will blend my metaphor of family with his of game so I can raise a family that does well in the game.

"I think I will focus on having Tom see me as a coach or mentor," she continued, "and put all of my efforts into reframing my approach in terms of his game metaphor. I am going to present myself as the guardian of the team, helping the players to move faster and make better 'scores.' I will enforce discipline and coach practice sessions so we can all play the game better. I'll make sure everyone has what they need to do their jobs well and play a winning game!"

Just then Beatrice placed their plates in front of them. "Will there be anything else?"

Eric smiled and said, "Thank you so much, Beatrice! I think we are fine for now."

Michelle nodded her agreement, and the pair ate with gusto.

5

Remembering Who You Are: Metaphors of Identity

KNOWING WHAT YOU WANT

As an organizational leader, you will find it critical to be able to motivate people to achieve desired tasks. A central task then becomes motivating others to help them to get what they want. But what do they really want? And for that matter, what do you really want? And how do you know that's what you want?

One of the most important implications of the Neurological Levels Model is that what people really want is to fulfill their values and identity. People evaluate everything based on whether or not their values and identity are being fulfilled. The essential drive for leaders is no different—leaders seek to fulfill their identities within the organizations they lead. In terms of the model of how we experience the world, identity is one of the filters that deletes, distorts, and generalizes information from the outside world. This is shown graphically in Figure 5.1.

In metaphors, two ideas are compared. The effect is to highlight certain aspects of the referent idea and subdue others. The primary function of the metaphor is to relate two domains of experience to create new meaning in the referent domain, as in this case business. In leadership metaphors, what concerns us more is the fact that metaphors both are outpictured into the world through our behaviors and carry values, beliefs, skills, and desired states that prescribe our desired reality. How metaphor results in a new view of the world is shown in Figure 5.2.

Values are the desirable qualities of things and events, not the actual things or events themselves. Value attribution is part of everyone's perception process, and it occurs mostly at a subconscious level. As a leader, when you acknowledge your follower's values, you have a tremendous amount of influence. The key is to create an organizational setting in which followers have the opportunity to fulfill their values and identities.

Values, however, are both contextual and derivative from identity. What is most important to a person stems from what metaphor the person is oper-

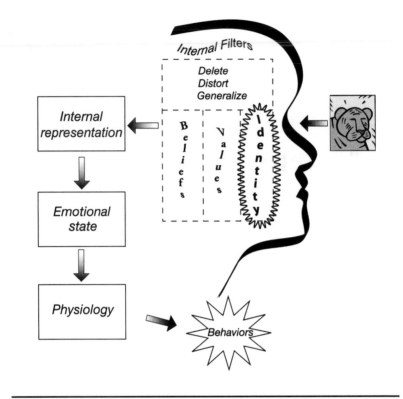

Figure 5.1   Identity.

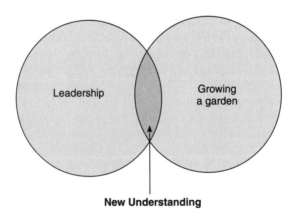

Figure 5.2   How metaphor works.

ating from at the moment and the context within which that metaphor is being played out. For example, if a person's metaphor is a game, values will most likely include fun and excitement. In contrast, if a person's metaphor is a machine, their values will most likely include precision and efficiency.

Leadership at the identity level can have the most far-reaching influence. For each of us in our leadership context, our underlying operating metaphor is driving our identity, beliefs, values, and capabilities. Our lives can be viewed as a mission to actualize our metaphor in the outer world of experience. We take a certain role and achieve a certain purpose, all within the larger context of reinforcing our metaphor of identity.

According to Charles Faulkner, the importance of understanding our living metaphors cannot be underestimated, and it is present in almost everything we do as well as in the possessions we bring to our lives:

> Once beyond survival and utility, everyone desires to express more of who they are. They do this by how they speak and how they act. And they can do this by what they own and what they use. Go to any superstore and you can see this in action. Once products become commodities, the differences between them are all about identity. Take a simple CD player as an example. Every consumer electronics maker produces them. And what are the different models? Sports, High Tech, Designer, Slimline, Multi-purpose—The names are practically identity niche markets as the individual buyers express themselves with their purchases. The CD player, their CD player, becomes a symbol of their lifestyle, an expression of their metaphor of identity. And it's that way with everything: a car is not just car, or a house a house, or clothes just clothes. We are, all of us, living as much in our imaginations as in the real world.

So what is a *metaphor,* exactly? According to Merriam-Webster, it is "a figure of speech in which a word or phrase literally denoting one kind of object or idea is used in place of another to suggest a likeness or analogy between them (as in drowning in money)." Metaphors describe something in terms of something else, and they are a fundamental mechanism of how human beings make meaning out of their world. They are the way we understand one thing in terms of another.

A metaphoric expression, then, is one in which one thing is stated as being another, such as "business is war." Now of course we realize that business and war are actually two separate activities; however, in making meaning of business by applying the concept of war, many insights and new meanings arise that simply weren't there before. The idea of business is simplified and vivified, and aspects of its complexity and uncertainty are reduced.

Your life metaphor is the primary coloring, if you will, of your perceptual filter, your lens of reality. It determines to a large extent what color will come out of your glass when you shine your light through it. It is how you make sense of your world, how you determine the roles that others play, and how you make meaning of the "plots" going on all around you. You have taken your understanding of one idea, expanded it to include the characteristics of another idea, and placed it into your consciousness as a literal truth for your world.

Leadership metaphors depend on the context in which they are expressed, your life metaphor, and what role you see for yourself within that life metaphor. For example, if you think life is a game and you see yourself as a highly skilled player, then this is most likely the metaphor you will carry over to your leadership situation. Leaders will generally have, however, one primary metaphor that expresses itself within their leadership context. We refer to this as an operating metaphor for leadership.

It is possible to have a leadership metaphor that is completely different from your life metaphor. You then need to determine what your exact leadership metaphor is, whether it differs from your life metaphor, and in what way you are using it to lead the organization. Most likely, your leadership metaphor will be (a) an extension of your life metaphor or (b) an extension of your business metaphor. You either will be bringing who you think you are to the leadership role or will be acting on a theme that you feel is true about business (if business is the context in which you are leading).

A leadership metaphor consists of a central theme around which is organized a group of beliefs, values and skills. A group of themes forms the basis of most of the current-day perceptions of business and leadership. These themes are that leadership (and business) is:

- Playing a game

- Growing a garden

- Fighting a war

- Parenting a family

- Going on an adventure or journey

- Operating a machine

- Caring for an animal (organism)

- Building a society (community)

- Being in a circus or amusement park

Each of these themes simultaneously emphasizes and downplays different aspects of your leadership experience. A note of caution is advisable here. We need to realize that metaphors, while they shed light on one aspect of a situation, at the same time hide other aspects that may influence the situation. These illuminating and obscuring characteristics of metaphors offer insight but also delete and distort information that may be useful. In determining the most effective approach, it is critical to know which aspects of a situation a metaphor highlights and which it obscures. Because metaphors also proscribe our desired reality, they need to be updated according to what we want to have happen in the world.

Projection also influences your leadership experience. It is defined as attributing one's own thoughts, motivations, desires, traits, and emotions to others. Projection is basically a defense mechanism that allows us to adapt to our environment.

According to Cheri Huber:

> When we look at the world and other people, we always see ourselves. I cannot see something that is not a part of me, that is, not a concept or experience that I have within me. If something happens around me for which I have no frame of reference, I will, rightly or wrongly, assign that experience to an already existing internal category of things with which I am more or less familiar; or I will not register that it happened at all . . . everything I encounter is a mirror of who I am.

In terms of leadership metaphor, when we project we place the people in our lives into certain categories based on our operating metaphor. We are acting as the central character in a play of our own choosing and unconsciously assigning supporting roles to others. Difficulties arise when we realize that everyone is assigning everyone else supporting roles. It is fine when roles interact with each other positively, which is fairly common because there is some overlap in metaphors as well as a wide interpretation of specific role functions. Difficulties may arise, however, when followers refuse to accept the roles you subconsciously chose for them. In this case, further communication or even changing your leadership metaphor may be necessary.

The importance of projection can be shown with an example. Let's say that your leadership metaphor is a game, and you are the coach of your team. Winning is everything and you do what it takes to get your team over the top. You view others in your organization as players, cheerleaders, and referees. Some of your followers, however, have the life metaphor of growing a garden. To them, winning has no meaning. It is all about growth, nurturing, and fit with the environment. They view others as visitors and friends and maybe a few pests!

In this case your organizational reward system may not have any meaning for the garden types. While you reward winning with prizes (bonuses and recognition), they are concerned with growth and caretaking. To you they may appear slow and unmotivated, but their internal frame of reference ascribes a different set of meanings and motivation levels to the rewards offered. To them, winning is simply irrelevant—it is not why they come to work. In such cases, wise leaders see the different metaphors and adjust reward systems to make sure all people are motivated equally.

The highlighting and obscuring effects of metaphors, as well as common leader and follower roles, are summarized in Table 5.1.

Table 5.1   Common leadership metaphors and their effects.

	Emphasizes	Obscures	Leader	Others
Playing a game (sports)	• Winning and losing • Playing by the rules • Teams • Speed and agility • Being a good sport • Fun	• Complex issues • Misplaced rewards • Personal growth and advancement • Lack of flexibility to respond to changing conditions	• Coach, team captain	• Spectators, players, opposing team, cheerleaders, mascot, referees
Growing a garden	• Growth • Nurturing • Diversity • Patience • Fit with environment • Maintenance and efficiency • Need for goals and objectives	• Inability to develop new internal strengths and skills • Need for speed and agility • Lack of precision	• Gardener, caretaker	• Visitors, friends, pests, nature, markets
Fighting a war	• Winning at all costs • Friends and enemies • Strategy • Hierarchy and coordination • Command and control • Heroes	• Cooperation • Lack of participation in decisions • Extreme actions • Need for growth and development • High risks	• General, officer	• Soldiers, prisoners, enemy, civilians, officers, allies, spies, casualties, targets
Parenting a family	• Development • Discipline and boundaries • Values and ethics • Nurturing • Responsibility • Stability • Lack of risk taking	• Inefficiency • Peer-to-peer relationships • Unwilling to involve some individuals or groups • Control	• Father, mother, guardian	• Children, relatives, friends, neighbors

(continued)

Table 5.1 Common leadership metaphors and their effects.

	Emphasizes	Obscures	Leader	Others
Going on a journey	• Destinations • Travel/movement • Adventure • Uncertainty • Preparedness • Length of time	• Lack of stability • Complex operations • Consolidating business success • Building community and stakeholder base	• Explorer, adventurer, captain, guide	• Travelers, agents, natives, inhabitants
Operating a machine	• Engineering • Rational enterprise • Goals and objectives • Structured behavior • Formal roles and responsibilities • Defined patterns of thinking • Precision and efficiency and workforce	• Human emotions, needs and wants • Flexibility to respond to changing conditions • Unquestioning attitude • Myopic viewpoints due to specialization • Distance between senior managers	• Designer, operator, bureaucrat	• Users, clients, production units, workers
Caring for animals (organisms)	• Survival and evolution • Domestication • Development and learning • Community and stakeholders • Unity and harmony, feelings	• Ability to shape own environment • Individual choice, contribution and uniqueness • Power and influence • Competition to survive	• Farmer, zookeeper, rancher	• Organisms, habitat, helpers

(continued)

(continued)

Table 5.1   Common leadership metaphors and their effects.

	Emphasizes	Obscures	Leader	Others
Building a society (community)	• Social structure and classes • Shared values and meanings • Proactive approach to future • Social basis of change • Interdependency and norms • Hidden values	• Coercion and political power • Self-created constraints and barriers • Ideological manipulation and propaganda	• Autocrats, statesman, chief, kahuna	• Community, electorate, society, opponents, elites, masses
Being in a circus or amusement park	• Fun, play and excitement • Variety, choice and creativity • Safety net • Ups and downs • Openness and information • Friends and visitors	• Continuity • Need to adapt to change • Lack of focus on key goals and objectives • Need for efficiency availability and practicality • Development and moving forward	• Ringleader, master of ceremonies, tour guide	• Friends or playmates, performers

LEADERSHIP LESSONS: DISCOVERING YOUR LEADERSHIP METAPHOR

The first step in discovering your leadership metaphor is to decide on a general theme. Is leadership playing a game or fighting a war? Once you have decided on a general theme, you will need to make it more specific. For example, if your theme is leadership is a game, then what kind of game is it? Is it football, soccer, car racing, wrestling? Or is it a foot race—a sprint or a marathon?

So where can we find your leadership metaphor? It is in the language you use and the objects you bring into your life. All you need to do is to listen carefully, or have someone else listen to you, and observe what you are wearing, what furnishings you have in your home or office, and how you structure your goals and measures of success.

Let's look at the following example. If a person's metaphor of leadership is that "leadership is war," then you might hear them saying something like the following:

The claims from our competitor's lawsuit are indefensible.

They attacked every weak point in our organization.

The analyst's criticisms were right on target.

I demolished his argument against raising salaries.

I have never won an argument with her.

If you use that strategy her group will wipe you out.

She shot down all of my ideas.

Making the metaphor more specific is just as important as identifying the general theme. In the game example, different games have vastly different rules and outcomes, and they require greatly different skills from the players. However, all players of athletic games share the needs for prowess, agility, and stamina at their particular game. The characteristics of the game will color your metaphor just as much as having the general theme of game. It is in the specifics of the game that the details of the theme become fleshed out and the theme becomes more real.

LEADERSHIP LESSONS: UNDERSTANDING YOUR LEADERSHIP PURPOSE

Once you have decided on a theme and a specific instance of that theme, you need to decide on your role. Why is this important? Because it is not enough to know your general leadership theme. While this theme provides you with a general sense of identity and helps you understand how the story of your leadership activities has unfolded, your role clarifies your specific identity as a leader—who you are and what you are doing. Your role also makes up half of your leadership purpose, which is the reason you are motivated to lead in the first place. Your leadership purpose shows how you fulfill your leadership metaphor.

Roles within themes are specific to each theme. For example, if leadership is a football game, are you the quarterback? A running back? A tight end? A referee? A coach? A spectator? If leadership is war, are you a general? A private? Another type of officer? A prisoner of war?

Your role is a specific instance of your identity within your leadership metaphor. Just as identifying the specific nature of your metaphor clarifies how it works, identifying your role clarifies how you act within your leadership theme. For example, if your metaphor is game, your theme is football, and your role is quarterback, you might see yourself doing such things as:

- Deciding on plays to use

- Taking action to move your team forward

- Receiving guidance from a coach

- Staying flexible and changing tactics to fit rapidly changing conditions

- Protecting yourself against the opposition by using strong linemen

- Making the big touchdown pass

When you understand your leadership purpose, the path you have taken as a leader will become clear, illuminated not only throughout your past but also casting light on your future direction.

The second half of your leadership purpose is to define your leadership function. Once you have decided upon your leadership role and function, you have then defined your leadership purpose, which in turn describes how you fulfill your leadership metaphor.

According to Charles Faulkner in *Creating Irresistible Influence with NLP,* there are five basic role functions, or areas of content around which role activities occur. These areas are shown graphically in Figure 5.3 and are as follows:

- *Information*—the drive to know and understand, measured by learning and knowledge

- *Things*—the drive to get or have, the process of acquiring, measured by wealth

- *Activities*—the drive to act and do, to accomplish things in the world, measured by production

- *People*—the drive to relate and connect with others, measured by the degree of belonging and community

- *Being*—the drive to be aware and feel, measured by experiences and records of being (photographs, stories)

What is interesting about role functions is that most people's leadership purpose involves a combination of several of them. For example, someone concerned with learning about being could be a leader of an organization that takes educational journeys (such as National Geographic). Or a person concerned with understanding people might be the leader of a teaching organization such as a college or university. There are many possibilities here, and the point is for you to figure out where your role functions lie and how you describe them to yourself.

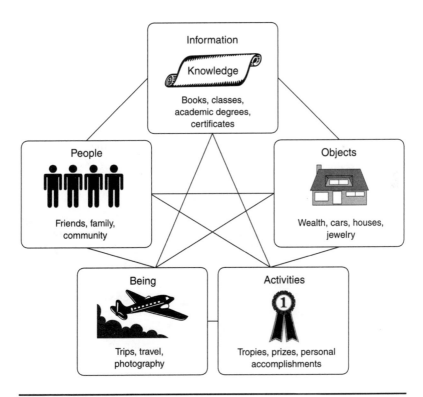

Figure 5.3   The five basic role functions.

You can also determine your role function by looking at the types of activities you routinely engage in and the types of objects with which you surround yourself. These objects tend to reinforce your purpose, as they are tangible expressions of its manifestation in the world.

What this is leading to is a leadership statement of purpose. The statement is phrased simply as follows:

I am a (role) _____ that/who (function) _____.

This is your leadership statement of purpose. With it you will understand your leadership direction and how you interact with your organization. Most important, when you link your metaphor, specific theme, role, and function, you understand why you have been acting a certain way in your leadership role—understanding the meaning of what you have been doing at a deep level. And it is in this understanding that you are able to move forward as an empowered leader, one with the key self-knowledge that will enable you to be effective in a variety of situations.

Some examples or leadership purposes are the following:

- I am a shining light who reflects your light into the world.
- I am the lighthouse beacon that draws people back home.
- I am the star player who wins the big games.
- I am the mirror that reflects your truth.
- I am the crashing wave that washes away the barriers.
- I am the team captain who motivates others to greatness.
- I am the wave of inspiration that moves you to shore.
- I am the imp that calls you forth onto the trampoline of life.

The process of defining your leadership metaphor and purpose is summarized in Figure 5.4. This process is the first step in becoming conscious of your map of reality and in decoding its important message for you. Leaders who understand their metaphors and leadership purposes are well-equipped to play a bigger game in their leadership arena, as they are on familiar terms with how they structure their world. They know how they are acting out their metaphor, what gives their leadership activities meaning, and what roles they really want those around them to play.

One of the most important aspects of leadership role and purpose is matching them to your given situation. Issues and problems that seem to arise even though you are working your hardest will most likely come from misalignment between your leadership context and your metaphor

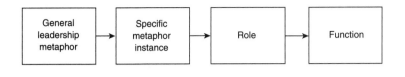

Figure 5.4   Defining your leadership metaphor.

and purpose. As a diagnostic tool, understanding your leadership metaphor and purpose can help you determine the source of any subpar performance. There is no one answer, however, for which leadership metaphor is right for any given context. The answer is to understand how your present metaphor is serving you, what performance it augments and diminishes, and how well it assists you in achieving your desired outcomes.

As an example, Susan is a trainer, workshop leader, and coach who runs a small business in Colorado. She is the leader of her company, responsible for making all business decisions and delivering services to clients. Her client style has emphasized fun, having the client do serious stuff in a way that's enjoyable. She views her job as making people laugh, and her primary differentiator is being fun and playful. She has had much success; however, lately she has been finding it difficult to set aside time for new product development. She is concerned that this lack of time for marketing, sales, and product development could hurt her business if she lost a major client.

When we looked at her identity, we came up with the following:

Metaphor: Life is a playground (Game)

Role: Activity Friend

Purpose: To call others forth to have fun and play with me (a combination of People, Being and Activity)

Values: Fun, happiness, excitement, play, harmony, tranquility

This metaphor highlights the following in her particular leadership context:

- Fun, play, and excitement
- Variety, choice, and creativity
- Friends and visitors

Susan keeps her business fresh by not playing the same game all the time. She is creative and always invents games to keep things fun and interesting. She enjoys meeting new people and getting them to play in her game. Her clients laugh with her all the time and seem to genuinely enjoy her coaching and training.

Her metaphor obscures the following in her particular leadership context:

- Lack of focus on key goals and objectives

- Need for efficiency and practicality

- Development and moving forward

Her business development efforts have been limited lately, and she is finding it difficult to set aside the time for key business goals. Her focus is almost exclusively on the clients and not on developing her web site, writing books, or marketing her services to new clients. She has taken on a lot of extra assignments just because they are so fun—reviewing client resumes, cover letters, business plans. Her focus on clients and her commitments to them have overshadowed her involvement with her business commitments and core business activities. She has not been building her business as much as operating from her current client base.

As a leader it is essential that you understand what your metaphor and purpose are, and how they relate to your situation. As in Susan's example above, leadership metaphors can yield results that on the surface seem to be successful but that upon deeper examination do not support all aspects of the organization. Remember that while you hold a certain metaphor and purpose, you, as a leader, are asking others to live within them. You are in effect creating a mental stage upon which you expect everyone else to adopt certain roles and characters and behave according to those roles. Realize that others may not share your metaphor and purpose, causing performance issues and conflicts.

Exercise 5.1 will help you understand your leadership metaphor. Once you understand it, you may recognize that it is not the most appropriate one for your current situation. If this is the case, Exercise 5.2 will show you how to change your metaphor so that you can adopt one that is more useful in achieving your outcomes.

This exercise is best done with a colleague asking you the questions and recording your answers. Find a quiet place to do the interview, and plan on taking 25 to 40 minutes to complete it.

1. Ask the person about a peak experience when he or she was a leader. *"What is a significant event in your leadership experience, one in which you felt really alive?"*

2. Ask questions about this peak experience and get the person to describe it in terms of what they saw, what they heard, how he or she felt at the time. After a person has talked a while about this experience, he or she will become more emotionally involved and his or her leadership metaphor will become available to his or her consciousness.

3. Once the person has fully entered into the experience, ask, *"What's important to you about this experience?"* Listen for common metaphors and metaphoric phrases, and write them down.

4. Ask the person *"What is leadership like for you?"* or *"What does leadership mean to you?"* These questions will often elicit his or her leadership metaphor directly.

5. After you have discovered his or her leadership metaphor, get him or her to express it in more detailed terms. For example, if leadership is a game, what type of game is it?

6. After you have discovered his or her specific metaphor instance, ask him or her *"What is your role in this _____ (metaphor name)?"* or *"What part do you play in this _____ (metaphor name)?"*

7. After you have discovered his or her role, ask him or her to look at Figure 3 and define his or her function. Ask, *"What is your purpose as a (role)? What do you do as a (role)?"*

Leadership Metaphor

Leadership is a _____

_____

_____

Specific Instance: My leadership is a _____

My role is a _____

My function is to

_____

Leadership Statement of Purpose

I am a (role) _____ that/who (function) _____

_____

Exercise 5.1   Defining your leadership metaphor.

This exercise will enable you to have more choice in how you respond to situations in which you feel you previously acted inappropriately. The purposes of this exercise are for you to:

1. Identify the metaphor for when you are leading and acting inappropriately.

2. Identify a second metaphor for how you would prefer to lead.

3. Explore how you can convert or evolve the first metaphor into the second.

4. Translate your insights into how you can change your behavior in your everyday life.

5. Rehearse this new behavior.

1. Identify a metaphor for when you are leading and acting inappropriately.

   a. Ask yourself, *"When I am leading and acting inappropriately, that's like what?"*

   b. On a separate piece of paper, draw the metaphor that comes to mind.

   c. Ask yourself the following questions so you get to know more about the symbols in the metaphor. For each part of the drawing, ask:

      "What kind of . . . ?"

      "Is there anything else about . . . ?"

Add new information to the drawing, and when you have all that you can get for now, go on to the second metaphor.

The purpose of these questions is to focus your attention on each part of the leadership metaphor so that you consider it in detail. You are working with personal symbols, and there are aspects to your metaphor that you did not consciously decide. These unexpected elements are often the places where a new kind of change can emerge.

2. Identify a second metaphor for how you would prefer to respond. This may come from a time prior to the problem response:

   a. Ask yourself, *"How I would prefer to respond is like what?"*

   b. Draw the metaphor that comes to mind.

   c. For each part of the drawing, ask yourself the following questions so you get to know more about the symbols in this metaphor:

      "What kind of . . . ?"

      "Is there anything else about . . . ?"

(continued)

Exercise 5.2   Changing your leadership metaphor.

(continued)

Add new information to the drawing, and when you have all that you can get for now, go to Step 3.

3. Explore how you can convert or evolve the first metaphor into the second:

   a. Place your drawings in front of you.

   b. Consider how Metaphor 1 can evolve into Metaphor 2.

   c. Notice:

      "What"s the first thing that needs to happen for Metaphor 1 to start becoming Metaphor 2?"

      "What's the last thing that needs to happen before Metaphor 1 becomes Metaphor 2?"

Take your time when completing Step 3. Consider all ideas that come to mind—the purpose is for you to discover something new. The path to change may not be simple and straightforward. It may take a number of intermediate stages for your metaphor to evolve. Accept all ideas that come to you, even if they seem bizarre (the land of metaphor is often closer to our dream world than to our everyday reality). You'll know when you've found the solution that's right for you, and it's usually a surprise.

4. Now that you have identified a way for Metaphor 1 to become Metaphor 2, how does this translate into actions in your everyday life? How will this information guide you next time you are in a similar situation?

5. Start getting used to this new way of leading. Rehearse being Metaphor 2 by embodying its characteristics:

   What is your posture?

   What do you feel inside?

   Where is your focus of attention?

   What do you say and how are you saying it?

Exercise 5.2   Changing your leadership metaphor.

Note: Adapted with permission from "The Magic of Metaphor" by Penny Tompkins and James Lawley, http://www.devco.demon.co.uk/Magic-of-Metaphor.html. For more on how to use metaphor and Clean Language see *Metaphors in Mind: Transformation through Symbolic Modelling* by James Lawley and Penny Tompkins, The Developing Company Press, 2000, ISBN 0-9538751-0-5.

6

A Walk on the Beach

After Eric and Michelle finished their lunch, Eric remarked "That was delicious Inferno Chili. Really hot and spicy, just the way I like it!"

Michelle noticed Eric was sweating profusely. She smiled and remembered when Eric had first tried Inferno Chili, and how he had complained because it was too hot. Now it seemed to be his favorite dish.

"I remember when you didn't like spicy food. What happened?"

Eric replied, "I read an article in a magazine about how good chili peppers are for you, and how they have important positive effects on your nervous system. I asked my doctor and he agreed, so ever since I have developed a liking for spicy food. I guess I just never knew how good chili peppers really were for you until I read that article."

Beatrice walked up to their table. "So how was everything? Can I get you anything else?"

Eric smiled. "No, I think we're done here," he said. "Just the check and we'll be on our way."

Beatrice cleared the plates. Eric excused himself to use the restroom, and Michelle was left alone to sip on her iced tea.

She looked around at the comfortable furnishings of the Greenery. What was it about this place that seemed to suit her so?

The table was in the back central part of the Greenery, in the main dining area. The furnishings were simple and warm, with plants hanging from the ceiling above each booth and paintings done in the classical romantic style by a local artist. Cherry paneling four feet high ran the length of all the walls in each room, and it was cleverly accented by a pale teal wallpaper. On the wall opposite Michelle were the owner's family photographs. In the background, an announcer on the television in the bar was saying something about an upcoming show on the Cooking Channel.

The napkins on each table were colored to match the walls, and Michelle breathed in the smell of barbecued steak wafting across the room.

She leaned back onto the cool brown leather of the booth, noticing how supple it seemed against her arm. She felt very comfortable sitting in the booth; across from her a white ceiling fan turned a slow, lazy dance.

Of course! This place reminded her of her grandmother's house, where she had gone many, many times as a child. Even some of their recipes were the same. That's why she felt so comfortable—it was like being in her family home! She fondly remembered her grandmother as a kind, caring woman who always had something delicious for them to eat whenever she and her parents would visit.

Eric returned from the restroom as Beatrice arrived with the check, saying, "Thank you so much for having lunch with us today."

Eric and Michelle each contributed their half of the bill and left a nice tip for Beatrice. Walking toward the entrance, Eric stopped at the hostess station to pay the bill while Michelle continued outside, where she stood next to a large fountain.

She felt the warm sun and heard the water splashing and the birds twittering in the trees. She breathed in the afternoon air, rich with salt from the sea. When Eric came outside, she said, "What a beautiful afternoon! What is your schedule like today?"

Eric replied that he had an important 2:30 meeting and that he needed to catch up on some paperwork after the meeting as he was behind on approving performance reviews. Michelle suggested they go for a walk on the beach close to SpeedyCo after they were finished with work as she still had some questions. Eric thought that would be a great idea, and they agreed to meet at 5:00 in the SpeedyCo parking lot. Since the beach was only a few blocks away, they would walk down.

He drove back to SpeedyCo, where Michelle got out of the car and walked back to her office. She had a lot of questions and looked forward to their walk that evening.

That afternoon, Michelle called home and told her husband, Randy, that she would be about an hour late, that she had some things she wanted to talk over with Eric. Randy replied that he would take care of dinner on his own and to tell Eric hello for him.

At 5:00 Michelle walked out of the main entrance and waved as she saw Eric drive into the SpeedyCo parking lot. He parked and walked over to where Michelle stood.

"How was your afternoon, Eric?"

"Really busy. I didn't finish everything I wanted to do, so tomorrow morning I will need to finish up those performance reviews. Are you ready to go?'

Michelle nodded her assent, and with that the pair strode across the parking lot and down the winding path toward the beach. The late afternoon sun was warm and a slight breeze was blowing in from the ocean, caressing their skin.

As they reached the beach they walked through a series of sand dunes over which gulls wheeled and cried. The sea grasses bent low in the breeze, which had become stronger as they neared the shoreline. Michelle noticed that the sun was halfway down the western sky, and thought to herself that they probably had no more than an hour or two until darkness overtook them.

The pair walked to the water's edge, where they removed their shoes and began walking south. The waves crashed and hissed along the sands, filling in their footprints. Palm trees swayed in the breeze, and gulls soared overhead.

"So what's on your mind, Michelle?" Eric said.

Michelle replied, "Ever since our conversation today about business metaphors I have been thinking about what matters most to me. I think I really like my metaphor of business as parenting. It explains a lot about how I have been behaving at SpeedyCo. I'm just not sure what it means for me in day-to-day life, though."

"So what's so important about business as parenting?" he asked.

"I think it's important for people to have rules and structures to help them succeed. Without guidelines where would we be? Also, I am really concerned about the people that work for me. I want them to grow and to protect their interests in the organization. I think it's key for me to act as a guardian and to influence upper levels of management so my people get the best."

Eric kicked at a piece of driftwood and splashed water onto the sand ahead. "You know, metaphors influence our values and beliefs. Each of us adopts a distinct set of values and beliefs based on our metaphor, and our role and purpose within the metaphor.

"For example," he said, "let's take the metaphor of 'business is a game,' much like the one your CEO, Tom, is using. In sports games, what is important is agility, speed, prowess, and whatever other skills can help you to win the game. What is also important is winning, as well as playing by the rules. Fun is another value that is common.

"So, if your leadership metaphor is sports, your role is coach, and your purpose is to build winning teams, then speed, agility, and fun would be important values. Also important would be knowing the rules and training players to bring out the best of their natural abilities."

Michelle smiled as she could see where this was leading.

Eric asked, "So how would you characterize yourself as a parent? Are you a strict parent or a nurturing parent?"

"I think I'm more of a strict parent. After all, that is how I was raised and it seemed to work out just fine for me. I think a stricter upbringing for children keeps them on the right path by setting boundaries and letting them know clearly what is right and wrong. It is how I raised my kids, and they are doing great now that they are on their own."

Eric said, "What you are saying about business as parenting is a mixture of values and beliefs. What happened at SpeedyCo was that Tom, when he hired you, echoed some of your core beliefs about business and that is why you were so excited about taking a job there. He also seemed to resonate with your business values."

Michelle was silent for a moment, listening to the sound of the surf and smelling the gentle salt breeze. She thought back to her interview with Tom and how motivated she had felt when he told her about how they needed someone to implement a quality structure for the company and how she would be given the opportunity to grow the position and the people who worked for her. It had all seemed so perfect!

She asked Eric, "So what is it about values and beliefs that makes them such an integral part of our day to day lives?"

As the two stood there gazing across the water, Eric said, "Values and beliefs are what guide us in making our day to day decisions. The only problem is, until we look at them and define what they mean for us, we are largely unconscious of them. What most people see as their virtues are actually their values.

"A major issue with values is, that when they are taken to extremes, they become hindrances to performance. What starts out as strength can quickly become weakness if we are not careful.

"For example, you value providing a structured environment for business. This value derives from your metaphor of business as parenting and is based on your belief that a stricter upbringing for children keeps them on the right path by setting boundaries and letting them know clearly what is right and wrong.

"In many situations this is an excellent value for business," he continued. "For organizations that don't understand how to structure their operations to achieve their goals, this value is very useful. Structure can guide them to establishing a coherent set of processes that work together to get a coordinated result.

"However, while structure is appropriate in many situations, it also has a down side, if you will. In today's complex and quickly changing business environment rules can become quickly outdated. Also, with some of today's larger organizations, just getting everyone trained to the same level of knowledge about the rules can be an overwhelming task. When you combine a huge effort to get everyone on the same set of rules, which are constantly changing, it becomes an exercise in frustration.

"Also, your value of structure needs to serve the greater metaphor within which you are operating. Sometimes the top management can see too much structure as limiting and not adding any value. For example, I think Tom sees it as slowing down his game—too many rules and not enough emphasis on playing. He wants to play his game hard and fast with just a few rules that everyone can easily understand."

The pair continued their walk in silence except for the sound of the waves crashing on the beach. After several minutes Michelle asked, "So what I need to do is to figure out how to honor my values and beliefs while adapting them to the situation?"

"Not exactly," Eric said. "While it is important that you honor your values to support your metaphor of identity, your beliefs are a little different. They are formed as a result of your experiences in life and are, for you, your truth. They can be misleading, as you generally derive them from a situation in which you have limited knowledge and perspective. In fact, it is almost impossible for you to know everything about a given situation—you would have to know what everyone involved was thinking and feeling and see things from their perspective, a sometimes impossible task. So our beliefs are our best attempt to make sense of reality."

Michelle laughed. "So how can I know if my beliefs are true?"

"The better question is to ask if your beliefs are what works for you to get what you want," he said. "The concept of truth can be a difficult one to fully understand, so let's leave it at that."

After a thoughtful pause Eric said, "Your belief about how a stricter upbringing for children keeps them on the right path by setting boundaries doesn't seem to be working for you in your business metaphor. Maybe it is too restrictive. You know there are parents who believe that nurturing and caring are most important because the child develops a better sense of grounding in the world as well as better developed self-esteem."

"I went to school with some of those people," she said. "They seemed much looser and tended to be creative types—artists, actresses, and writers. It seemed like their personal lives were kind of a mess, though."

"So the main thing about beliefs is that you realize they are your personal version of reality. In fact, I would venture a guess that Tom has a very different belief about how people in a business should be treated, probably more like players in a league. I bet he values training and practice and believes that winning is everything and teamwork yields the best results.

"So what we could do is figure out a way to integrate both of your core beliefs to help them work together. I think there is enough overlap so you can do this. What do you think would work for you?"

"Maybe I've taken my belief a bit too far," she said. "Maybe I can still believe that a stricter upbringing is better because it lets them know the rules of the game and develop winning strategies based on living these rules on a daily basis. I guess I need to stress how the rules can be used to be successful and to win the game.

"I need to flip my perspective on rules and boundaries and see them in a more positive light. I can emphasize on how the rules fit together to make everyone a better team player. Knowledge is a good thing, and knowing the rules better than the competition makes our team more effective. We can develop winning strategies that allow us to beat the competition. I can be the guardian of the team by making sure everyone knows what the rules really mean and how they can use them to their advantage to play the best game they can."

Eric beamed and said, "Now that's the ticket!"

The pair walked for a few minutes, just feeling the spray from the waves on their faces and the water and sand running between their toes. Michelle felt as though an enormous weight had shifted within her, and she was feeling a little off-balance and somewhat hungry. When she told Eric how she was feeling, he remarked that he, too, needed to eat something and suggested they finish out the day with dinner at La Fontaine, a French restaurant with a reputation for excellent dishes.

The pair turned around to walk back to Eric's car. Michelle thought to herself what a powerful day this had been and how valuable her new insights were. They walked into a sunset glowing in crimson and orange, and the waves seemed to quiet down as the curtain of evening closed around them.

7

What Matters Most:
Values and Beliefs

KNOWING WHAT IS IMPORTANT

Values and beliefs arise from the leadership metaphor you are using in any particular situation, which we can also call your operating metaphor. This metaphor carries with it certain presuppositions, assumptions, values and beliefs based on to what it is. Just as we have already seen with metaphors, values and beliefs come in many flavors, sizes and shapes. Two examples at a cultural level will help to illustrate how values and beliefs can be embedded in an operating metaphor.

First, in Japan, there is a popular metaphor that the nail that sticks up gets pounded first. The value embedded is that it's important to be like everyone else. The supporting belief is that conformity is best. In the United States, by contrast, a popular metaphor is that the squeaky wheel gets the grease. The embedded value is that it's important to be loud, noisy, and colorful. The supporting belief is that it is okay to make noise and be loud—after all, you need some grease!

Values can be thought of as states of being that you want to experience because they reinforce your operating metaphor. They can also be thought of as a deep knowing, trust or conviction in an aspect of life that you consider to be desirable and inherently worthwhile. The key to understanding values is to realize that, until you consciously explore, distinguish, and clearly delineate your personal values, you will not be able to orient your professional life around them.

Your leadership metaphor determines the overall size and shape of your perceptual map of reality. Values may also be thought of as part of your perceptual map, the color of your filter to the external world. When you look through a colored filter, let's say red, certain other colors are highlighted and certain other ones are suppressed. Your values are the areas of your life that are highlighted as you view the world through your perceptual filter.

What is important and true shines through and resonates with your leadership metaphor. This is shown graphically in Figure 7.1.

Understanding our set of personal values helps us build the credibility and trust that facilitate leadership. The most challenging times for leaders are when they must lead others into an unknown space, leading innovation, and managing change. Effective leaders are able to persuade their followers to take a leap of faith and follow them into the undefined territories.

But why would people willingly follow someone into the unknown? Because the person has established him or herself as a leader by building trust. Trust is the certain knowing that supports taking risks and opening yourself and being vulnerable. We are more inclined to trust people when we understand their values and observe that their actions are congruent with those values, because we can reliably predict how they will act. We trust what we understand and know to be true based on what we observe.

So a central task for all leaders, then, is to identify the values that are most important to them. The next step is to find the personal courage to live

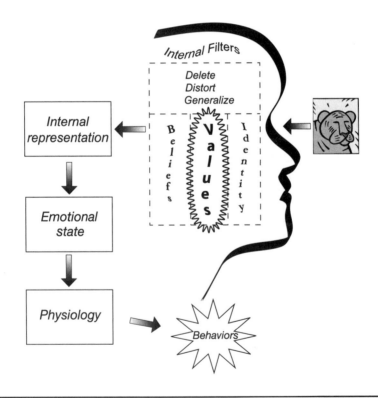

Figure 7.1 Values as perceptual filters.

these values in all situations. Courage demands that we draw on our inner reserves of strength. It requires us to commit to a course of action with unwavering dedication. To build trust, leaders must summon courage and strength, drawing on their inner reserve of power so they live their values at all times.

Values, in and of themselves, are only half of the picture. It is just as important to support these values with elucidated beliefs. Beliefs are generalizations that impact your behaviors. They arise from something you induce to be true based on an experience or set of experiences that you have had. They are versions of personal truths about you and the world around you. Usually, a belief directly supports a value, in that values are what give your beliefs and experiences meaning. Values are the higher level positive intentions that the belief has been established in order to support.

For example, you may have a value of professionalism. That is to say professionalism is important to you in your leadership metaphor, role and purpose. But what does professionalism mean exactly? The word by itself is a nominalization, and does not possess discrete meaning for every individual. Rather, each person reads into the word what he or she believes to be true about professionalism.

To make your value of professionalism clear to yourself and to others in your leadership circle, you may further define it as working with competence, creativity, and joy, or observing precisely and setting high standards. Or even knowing your limits and modeling excellence.

Another example would be having the value of renewal. You might believe that renewal, for you, is being in the natural world and connecting with the life force of nature. However, someone else may have this same value and find renewal in being with their close family and connecting on a deep emotional level with them. In this case it is the value that is the same but it is the underlying belief that differs. We see that beliefs are a further expression and detailing of a value for a particular person based on their experience and leadership purpose.

Beliefs exist in several forms, one of which is a generalization about a value and your identity. Beliefs can also be about the world around you, your behavior, and your capabilities. From an inner leadership perspective, this book concerns itself with beliefs about your values, identity, capabilities, and behavior.

Beliefs about your behaviors and capabilities can be either limiting or fostering—they can inhibit you getting what you want or help you to get it. Several limiting beliefs are commonly found, such as something's wrong with me, I am not okay, I can't learn it, and I can't do it. Note that these beliefs, while not true in the general sense, are true for the individuals who possess them and will severely restrict what is possible for them in their lives.

Table 7.1   List of possible values.

• Achievement	• Friendships	• Pleasure
• Advancement and promotion	• Growth	• Play
	• Happiness	• Power and authority
• Adventure	• Having a family	• Privacy
• Affection (love and caring)	• Helping other people	• Prosperity
	• Helping society	• Prosperity
• Arts	• Honesty	• Public service
• Challenge	• Independence	• Purity
• Change and variety	• Influencing others	• Quality of what I take part in
• Cleanliness	• Inner harmony	• Quality relationships
• Close relationships	• Integrity	• Recognition (respect from others, status)
• Community	• Intimacy	
• Communication	• Intellectual status	• Religion
• Competence	• Involvement	• Respect
• Competition	• Knowledge	• Reputation
• Contribution	• Leadership	• Responsibility and accountability
• Cooperation	• Location	
• Country	• Loyalty	• Security
• Creativity	• Market position	• Self-respect
• Decisiveness	• Meaningful work	• Serenity
• Democracy	• Merit	• Spirituality
• Ecological awareness	• Money	• Sophistication
• Economic security	• Nature	• Stability
• Effectiveness	• Being with people who are open and honest	• Status
• Efficiency		• Supervising others
• Environment	• Order (stability, conformity)	• Time freedom
• Ethical practice		• Tradition
• Excellence	• Peace	• Truth
• Excitement	• Personal Growth	• Wealth
• Fame	• Physical beauty	• Wisdom
• Freedom	• Physical challenge	• Work under pressure

Fostering beliefs, on the other hand, enable you to progress forward into what is possible for you and expand who you are in the world. Some examples might be these: I can do it, I am capable, I can make a difference in the world, I can change, and the world is a friendly place.

Your beliefs, whether limiting or fostering, will greatly influence your success as a leader. You will be energized to the degree that you believe the following to support your leadership agenda (vision, strategy, alignment, and motivation):

- I deserve to achieve this agenda (self-worth).

- I have the capabilities to achieve this agenda.

- I have clearly defined what has to be done and it is appropriate for the situation.

- It is possible for me to achieve the agenda.

- The agenda is valuable and worth it.

So some evaluation of self-oriented beliefs in reference to your leadership agenda is in order. This topic is explored in much greater detail in Chapter 14. For now, it will be sufficient for you to examine and list out your values and their supporting beliefs, so that you have a clear idea how you are reinforcing your leadership metaphor.

LEADERSHIP LESSONS: ARTICULATING YOUR VALUES AND SUPPORTING BELIEFS

It's important to fully define your values and their supporting beliefs in writing. This is because they are mostly subconscious, and it will take you some time and concerted effort to unearth them. Your effort needs to be focused on relaxing and allowing them to emerge. As our subconscious guides, our values and beliefs have many forms, have come from many places, and can even conflict with one another. The process of writing them out slows down your conscious mind so that your values and beliefs can emerge in detail, and you get a clear picture of what your map of reality is like. A list of possible values is shown in Table 7.1, and some examples of fully defined values are shown in Table 7.2.

The goal of articulating your values and supporting beliefs is to arrive at a set of statements that resonate with you deeply. Remember, you are listing and defining your generalizations about your identity and leadership purpose. You should examine your value and belief matrix and make sure each value and belief fulfills the following three criteria:

1. *The value/belief is positively stated.* For example, "I can learn to enjoy advanced statistics."

2. *The value/belief needs to be a process, not a goal.* For example, "I can reach and maintain my desired salary," not "I will make $100,000 per year."

3. *The value/belief fits with all other values/beliefs and there is no conflict.* To ascertain whether conflict exists, ask yourself what will happen as this value/belief is manifested in your life.

Value 1: Authenticity—I speak the truth from my heart to others and let right actions flow from my innermost being.

Supporting beliefs:
• If I am dishonest it will hurt everyone involved.
• Honesty is the best policy.
• When I tell the truth then I don't have to remember any stories or lies.

Value 2: Beauty—I appreciate beauty and grace in all forms, and I create beautiful environments that speak to my soul.

Supporting beliefs:
• Beauty makes things more enjoyable.
• A beautiful environment is more balanced and productive.
• Beauty creates more beauty.

Value 3: Balance—I keep all parts of my life in harmonious balance and right relationship with each other.

Supporting beliefs:
• Balance gives me the ability to look at my life clearly.
• Balance is the key to success.
• Right relationship enables me to be more productive and satisfied.

Figure 7.2 Examples of values and beliefs.

Exercise 7.1 is designed for you to arrive at a matrix of values that support your leadership purpose and also derive a set of beliefs that support those values. This document may take many sittings to complete, so remember that an important benefit is learning the process of communicating with your subconscious. This requires that you relax and center yourself, listening to the small voice within you instead of the daily chatter and external cacophony with which you are familiar. It is a different approach to listening, one that in the context of this exercise yields both intrinsic and extrinsic rewards.

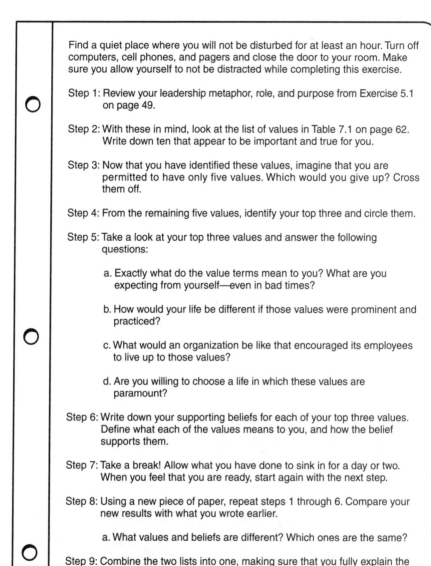

Find a quiet place where you will not be disturbed for at least an hour. Turn off computers, cell phones, and pagers and close the door to your room. Make sure you allow yourself to not be distracted while completing this exercise.

Step 1: Review your leadership metaphor, role, and purpose from Exercise 5.1 on page 49.

Step 2: With these in mind, look at the list of values in Table 7.1 on page 62. Write down ten that appear to be important and true for you.

Step 3: Now that you have identified these values, imagine that you are permitted to have only five values. Which would you give up? Cross them off.

Step 4: From the remaining five values, identify your top three and circle them.

Step 5: Take a look at your top three values and answer the following questions:

   a. Exactly what do the value terms mean to you? What are you expecting from yourself—even in bad times?

   b. How would your life be different if those values were prominent and practiced?

   c. What would an organization be like that encouraged its employees to live up to those values?

   d. Are you willing to choose a life in which these values are paramount?

Step 6: Write down your supporting beliefs for each of your top three values. Define what each of the values means to you, and how the belief supports them.

Step 7: Take a break! Allow what you have done to sink in for a day or two. When you feel that you are ready, start again with the next step.

Step 8: Using a new piece of paper, repeat steps 1 through 6. Compare your new results with what you wrote earlier.

   a. What values and beliefs are different? Which ones are the same?

Step 9: Combine the two lists into one, making sure that you fully explain the supporting belief for each value.

Exercise 7.1   Defining your values and beliefs.

SECTION 3

THE DOING OF LEADERSHIP

8

What Leaders Really Do

Most likely, you have a good idea of what you would like to do and what you would like to accomplish as a leader. Now you also know why—you are living your leadership metaphor and purpose and are acting in accordance with your values and beliefs. Behind every desire is a reason, and behind every reason is a purpose. Connect your desire with your leadership purpose, and you'll connect with the strength necessary to achieve that desire.

Achievement requires much effort and commitment, time, energy, and persistence. You're absolutely capable of all that and more when there's a real, meaningful purpose to what you're doing. But without a clear leadership purpose, you're likely to become discouraged, bored, or frustrated and give up. By contrast, with a strong, driving purpose behind your leadership efforts you'll find a way to work through any challenge.

The more you know about yourself and about what drives you, the more effective every effort and every moment will become. Know why, and the road to your dreams will unfold with every step you take.

The first part of this book was about this *why*. It concerned itself with the being of leadership—identifying the strong, driving purpose that exists outside of any particular time or space. The focus was on two key aspects of your internal map of reality: your leadership metaphor and your values and beliefs. We saw that they become, in effect, a stained-glass window through which you view the world and through which you project yourself out into the world. They create the strong, driving purpose that propels you toward success.

This next part of the book concerns itself with the doing of leadership—the actions that leaders take within themselves and in their organizations. It is concerned with movement and activity. Once you have connected with your leadership purpose, you will need certain capabilities to execute the art of leadership flawlessly in the world. This is what the second section of the book is about—capabilities for success.

There are lots of ways to interpret the actions of leaders, but according to John Kotter of the Harvard Business School, leaders are involved with only three primary activities (shown in Figure 8.1):

- Setting direction and strategy

- Aligning people

- Motivating and inspiring people

Although this model was developed in reference to the external actions leaders take, it is equally applicable to the internal actions necessary for excellent leadership. In fact, these three areas of emphasis provide an overall "inner" framework of capabilities that must exist in order to achieve performance excellence. This inner framework is shown in Figure 8.2.

As we address each capability in turn, we focus on what is required for extraordinary leadership. We see that setting direction requires defining well-formed outcomes; that aligning people requires developing and applying the skills of emotional intelligence; and that motivating and inspiring people requires self-motivation through leadership belief evaluation. Through these skills, the themes of alignment and congruence play themselves out.

The organizational leader is interested in aligning the beliefs and values of people with the overall goals and vision of the organization. In the leadership role you can bring about change by providing direction, by setting an example, by motivating through inspiration, and by building teams based on

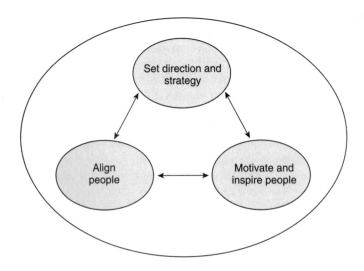

Figure 8.1   The work of leaders.

respect and trust. A leader is focused on results rather than methods, systems, and procedures. Leaders ask themselves, "For what purpose?" and "What are the consequences for the system as a whole?"

The same is true for "inner" leaders! You must ask yourself "For what purpose?" and "What are the consequences for my life as a whole?" You need to align your leadership metaphor, purpose, values, beliefs, capabilities, and actions with your overall outcomes in order to be congruent. You must manage your emotions successfully in order to effectively direct yourself toward positive behaviors. Finally, you have to clearly articulate your dream so you experience optimism, passion, and a sense of desire that will carry you through the tough times. Congruency, emotional management, and passion then become the inner foundations for successful leadership (Figure 8.2).

As we move past self-knowledge into the doing of leadership, the example of Monty Roberts, the "horse whisperer," can serve as a guide to the second part of this book. Monty identifies himself as "the man who listens to horses." Using a method involving kindness and communication, he can start a horse to saddle, bridle, and rider in an average of 30 minutes. "I don't 'break' horses in 30 minutes, I 'start' them," he says. "I want the horse on my team."

Monty's method involves horse and trainer establishing a bond of communication and trust. "You must somehow understand that we as horsemen can do very little to teach the horse. What we can do is to create an environment in which he can learn." Monty says. "We hear that 'actions speak

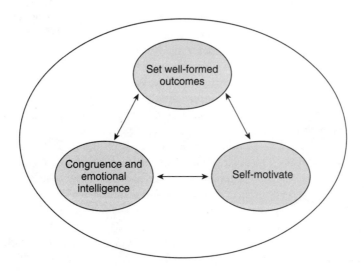

Figure 8.2   The inner work of leaders.

louder than words,' but generally we do not live by it too successfully. The horse has a very effective, involved and discernible nonverbal language. The incredible thing about this language is that these animals need no interpreters. Around the world they are understood by all of 'EQUUS,' one common language that has been around for millions of years."

The central idea in the story of Monty Roberts is that although horses may run away from strange humans at the slightest provocation, they follow and "join up" with interesting humans who appear to pose no threat to them. We share with horses a desire to join up and be part of something. We shy away from forceful commands for loyalty and commitment, but we congregate around focal points where "cool stuff" seems either to be happening or about to happen. Effective leaders work with our desire to involve ourselves with others in interesting work and exciting projects—projects that motivate us and ignite our passions. Effective leaders influence and seduce, rather than command, and serve as "attractors," as complexity scientists put it—the embodiment of attractive energy, the center of the horde.

But leaders can be attractive, in this sense, only when they themselves are truly aligned and congruent. Alignment and congruency start from the inside. You must be sure of your leadership metaphor and purpose, understand and project your values and capabilities, and ensure that these inner resources fully agree with one another. In short, there is no substitute for being an authentic and coherent person. That is not to say you have to be perfect. Your faults don't matter if you know what you are good at, understand your weaknesses, and lead authentically. Just as you need to look like you know where you're going and it looks like a good place to go before horses will follow, so too today's leaders need a high degree of internal alignment before they start asking others to follow them. The mandate is obvious: inner alignment precedes outer success.

The process of internal alignment can also be compared to a resonating tuning fork. Once the fork is struck, it vibrates, producing a tone. Your emotional tone is produced as an inner state based on how you perceive the world through the filter of your metaphor, values, and beliefs. An external event happens (or you do something), it is passed through your map of reality and you create an emotional response based on the meaning that you assign to the event. The goals of alignment are to understand your map and how it generates your emotional state, to gain awareness of your dominant emotional tone, and to manage it so that you are consistently in the expansive register.

Expansive emotions are contagious and greatly influence and reinforce personal motivation and drive. They enable your actions in the world to "flow" almost effortlessly. Once aligned internally, you can act with determination, passion, and vigor.

The context of leadership capabilities is also important. What leaders do is prepare organizations for change and help people cope as they struggle through it. As the rate of change in our world increases, doing what was done in the past is no longer a formula for success. In adapting to change, leaders must constantly update their maps of reality as well as their capabilities. More change requires more leadership, and more leadership requires greater self-awareness and leadership skills. An internally aligned leader with an outdated map and skill set will most likely not take the organization where it needs to go.

A good place to start is with the awareness and skills set forth in this book. These are your foundation for leadership success. As events and situations change, you can add to or evolve these so that you will continue to be perceived as an authentic person. It is in your authenticity and integrity that you will find your wellspring of leadership power.

9

Dinner at La Fontaine

On the way to La Fontaine, Michelle again called home to speak with her husband, Randy. He told her that he had eaten with a friend and was just relaxing in the den. Michelle smiled and thanked Randy, letting him know that she would be about another hour or two getting home as she and Eric had decided to have dinner. Randy laughed and said that she must really be onto something, and to have a good meal. Michelle hung up the phone, thinking that she could always depend on Randy to fill in at home when she had a pressing business appointment.

As he pulled into the parking lot at La Fontaine, Eric noticed that the restaurant had installed new walkway lights. After parking the car, Eric and Michelle walked across the lot and stood for a minute under the massive palm trees that braced the entrance to the courtyard. Starting from ground level and climbing high up into the trees, little white lights were splayed around the trunks and branches. They could hear water trickling from a fountain and felt the warm breeze as it moved across the courtyard.

Michelle thought to herself that this was a nice place and that the new owners had done an admirable job fixing up the outside. They walked through the courtyard and into the lobby, where they were greeted by a courteous young man. Michelle looked around at the interior and noticed more changes. It seemed as though the inside was much more subdued in greens and blues than before, with new paintings in the Impressionist style.

"I hope the food is just as good here as I remember it," she said to Eric as they walked to their table. Eric turned and nodded his assent. They were seated in the center of the room next to a large water sculpture, and the tinkling sound of the flowing water reminded Michelle of little voices talking and singing together.

As they picked up the menus, both of them realized that something was radically different—the menus were written entirely in French! Michelle glanced at Eric and said, "I hope they can help us here, as my French is not very good."

Eric motioned to a waiter who seemed to be ignoring them. He caught the waiter's eye, and with a look of mild disgust the waiter came over to the table. "Yes, monsieur?" he said grudgingly.

Eric asked if he could explain the menu as their French was not very good. The surly waiter then proceeded, brusquely and in a very heavy French accent, to explain the items on the menu. The pair exchanged incredulous glances—was this waiter for real?

After he had finished, both Eric and Michelle realized that they were no closer to understanding the menu than when they had first looked at it. Eric asked the waiter for two glasses of red wine and a bottle of mineral water while they thought about their meal choices. The waiter huffed, "Very well," and walked off to get their drinks.

Eric turned to Michelle and said, "I can't understand what this menu says. Do you know what you want to eat?"

Michelle replied, "I have no idea what is on this new menu and I couldn't understand what the waiter was saying; he spoke so fast and had such a heavy accent. I think I am just going to ask for something by price so at least I know what I will be paying."

"But you have no idea what you will be eating—what if you order something you don't like?"

Michelle replied, "I like most everything and besides, this is supposed to be a good restaurant, so anything they have should be good."

The waiter returned with their drinks and asked them what they would like for dinner. Each in turn pointed to an item on the menu. The waiter studiously wrote down their order and then left them to their conversation.

Eric and Michelle sampled their wine, which was an excellent French merlot.

Michelle began the discussion. "You know, I was wondering what I need to do to make my customer service project a success at work. I am at the point where I am feeling frustrated and don't know where to move ahead. Although now I understand myself at a much deeper level, I am having trouble figuring out what to do next."

Eric said, "Well, it all depends on what you mean by a success. What do you really want for this project?"

"I don't want any problems, and I don't want any more delays in everyone's training. I don't want the systems to keep having so many problems, and I don't want the procedures to remain in their current state of inaccuracy and relative disrepair. I want SpeedyCo to get rid of its unsatisfied customers."

"Well, maybe you need to rethink what you want in this case. How about stating what you want in the positive?"

"I want everything to go smoothly and for the training to proceed without any further delays," she said. "I want the systems to work perfectly and the procedures to be revised to be accurate and complete. I want SpeedyCo to improve its customer satisfaction rating by at least 20 percent. Is that positive enough?"

"Yes, yes, indeed," Eric said with a laugh. "I think so. But how much of what you want can you actually control yourself?"

"That's a great question. Now that I think about it, I am realizing that very little of what I want for this project is in my direct control. I have been depending on my influence on others to get this project completed."

"The key here is for you to specify your goal, or outcome, in terms of what you can directly control," Eric said. "The way to lead your project is to get everyone else to do the same, with you serving as an example. When you don't specify your goals in terms of what you can control, you become stuck, just like you are now."

Michelle smiled and said, "I thought that there was a better way to go about things. There are quite a few things I can control directly. However, in my current position, most of what I do is matrix manage and influence people directly. I guess that's why it's so important to get everyone working within their span of control so we can be realistic about project goals."

"How will you know when you have achieved what you want?" Eric said. "Have you decided on how to specify your deliverables?"

Michelle took a sip of her wine and responded sheepishly. "You know, I never really specified them in any detail. I just thought that everyone could tell by what I was asking them to do. I guess I need to write a more detailed project plan and specify each deliverable in detail, including the person responsible, and make sure they can actually perform the task I am asking them to do."

Eric drank deeply of his wine and exclaimed, "Exactly! Also, you will need to take a look at each task and deliverable to make sure that they are appropriate in scope. That is, they are achievable in a reasonable amount of time and with a reasonable amount of effort. The real secret is, however, to make sure that each task directly supports the overall goal of the project. It's really easy to get sidetracked in these large projects and lose sight of the larger goal."

Michelle also took a deep swallow of her wine. She said, "I never thought about it like that. I just put together a few basic tasks and thought that everyone would understand what was necessary. I guess I really need to revisit my entire project to make sure all the tasks fit with one another and support the overall project goals. I really need to look at how I specified success, though. That's where I think I left too much open to interpretation.

"For right now, though, I am going to focus on my training program. I can control the amount and type of training, how it will be delivered, and by whom. I can also control how the outcomes will be measured. I can influence how the training is perceived by top management as well as everybody else."

Just then the waiter walked to their table and served their food. Eric and Michelle exchanged looks of horror. What had they ordered?

Michelle's dinner was a large pile of greens surrounded by circular strips of meat, interspersed with what looked like yellow and red coat buttons. Eric's eyes opened wide as he beheld a small hairless mammal with long ears, cooked in its entirety and splayed across a bed of lettuce.

They both took another large swallow of their wine.

Eric said, "I guess we needed to be more specific about what we ordered. Talk about outcomes! What is this?"

Michelle replied, "I have no idea what we ordered. It sure smells good, though. I guess this will teach us about clearly understanding and asking for what you want. Are you ready to eat it?"

Eric motioned to the waiter and ordered a full bottle of wine.

"Let's give this our best try. I'm sure with enough wine it will be delicious," he said dryly.

And with that, the pair set about devouring their repast in its entirety.

10

Orientation: Identifying Well-Formed Outcomes

THE IMPORTANCE OF OUTCOMES

One of the key principles of our human world is that mental creation precedes physical creation. Many people gain an idea of who they are and what they want from the opinions, perceptions, and paradigms of the people around them. They allow circumstances, conditioning, and the social mirror to mold what they want to achieve.

Effective leaders shape their own future. Instead of letting other people or circumstances determine what they want, they mentally visualize and then physically create their own positive results. What they picture in their mind shapes the entirety of their lives.

Once your vision of what you want it is truly within you, it will begin to expand throughout your experience. The vision you create within you can never be lost. Every improvement you make in the quality of your vision will always be with you. The dreams that you can make real are the dreams that come from the deepest part of you. Nurture and build them first within you, and they'll become so powerful as to be undeniable.

When what is within you is clear and well defined, the positive energy will flow outward and can touch every part of your life. And nothing outside you can diminish it. Others can point the way and give encouragement. Yet ultimately, you are responsible for taking good care of your inner life and visualizing what it is you truly want.

Your mind may be compared to a garden. Whether it is intelligently cultivated or allowed to run wild, it will bring forth new growth. Just as gardeners cultivate their plots, keeping the weeds in control and fostering those plants that are truly desired, so you can tend the garden of your mind. By pursuing this process you will discover that you are the master gardener of your own psyche, the director of your life. The key is clearly specifying what type of plants you want to grow!

LEADERSHIP LESSONS: DEFINING WHAT YOU WANT

The first step to defining what you want is to ask yourself the question "What do I want?" This critical first step can sometimes be dismissed as either not important or not relevant. Too often leaders will assume an externally imposed goal as valid without ever considering if this is what they truly want. To do so obviates an essential leadership responsibility—taking personal responsibility for an outcome. Determining what is truly wanted is foundational to personal leadership effectiveness.

This seemingly simple first step will often resolve 80 percent of the issues associated with a program or leadership initiative. It still astounds me how many instances I encounter in which the person has not decided what they want. Just knowing what you want and specifying it clearly is the foundation for successfully getting it. In those cases in which you know exactly what it is that you want, gaining agreement with your followers is on a much surer footing—they know what it is they are agreeing to, and have an understanding of where you as a leader are headed.

The next step is to structure what you want in terms of the well-formedness conditions. It is essential to state what you want in a way that will catalyze its achievement. While fuzzy logic may be acceptable for solving certain math problems, it is certainly not the way to ensure that you actually achieve what you want. By clearly specifying what you want in unambiguous terms, it crystallizes your vision and slows it to spring forth as an accurate representation of your originating thought.

What we are really dealing with here are the concepts of focus and precision. When you know what you want, you can bring it into clarity as you apply the well-formedness conditions and reveal its finer details, as if focusing a camera lens on an object. In the preciseness of the way your goal is stated will you find its richness and catalyze its achievement in the outer world.

If we look at an out-of-focus picture, we may see just a large orange shape with indistinct outlines and shading. We can't tell what the subject is. An orange? A pumpkin? A reflection of leaves on water? As we bring the picture into focus, we see that it is indeed an orange in a fruit basket.

Analogous to the out-of-focus picture, goals and desires that are not clearly defined can result in any one of several things manifesting in our lives. We could get an orange, or a pumpkin, or leaves on water. It is up to you as a leader to clearly specify your outcomes so you can manifest them exactly as you have conceived of them. Knowing exactly what you want, from the viewpoint of the inner leader, is essential to getting it.

Knowing what you want and stating it clearly, however, are two different matters. The former requires self-awareness, while the latter requires you to make sure the goal fulfills a set of well-formedness conditions. Once you have defined in a general way what you want, you sharpen your picture by applying the well-formedness conditions. In this way you know exactly what it is you desire, and there is a much greater chance that it will come to pass in exactly the way you have specified.

Deletion, distortion, and generalization work on statements heard and are relevant to specifying well-formed outcomes. When we hear "Don't look behind that door," what do we do? We immediately look behind the door. Our subconscious minds hear the second part of the statement more loudly than the first, and we generate a behavior according to what we actually hear. This principle of selective hearing is why it is important to state all desired outcomes or goals in the positive—"I want X," not "I don't want Y." When you say, "I don't want Y," your subconscious mind focuses on Y and it becomes more likely that Y will appear in your life.

There is also another trap here—the trap of negativity. When you focus on what you don't want, you run the risk of devolving into complaining about things rather than setting a course of action that will resolve a situation. This focus drains energy and emphasizes the past, rather than what you want to have happen. You risk becoming stuck in the quagmire of contractive emotions, which can slow your goal achievement efforts to a halt. The imperative is to state what you want in positive terms.

Another critical part of a well-formed outcome is control. Stating goals that involve activities over which you have no control is setting yourself up for failure and frustration. Your goals need to reflect matters over which you have direct control and authority. This subtle characteristic of goals is also the one most likely to be causing you difficulties. Look at each outcome and determine whether it is indeed something over which you have direct control, whether what you do or do not do will affect its achievement, or whether it depends on the actions of others.

Outcomes that involve activities that you can perform have a much greater chance of becoming reality that those that require other people to perform certain tasks, especially if you have no influence or authority over those people. Your goals should reflect what you can do to directly influence their achievement.

For example, you may have a goal to have a better relationship with your staff. This is not entirely controllable by you, as the staff has their own set of relationship criteria and personal values. This goal would be better restated as a set of relationship-building activities that you will undertake on your own and with your staff, such as personal development and team-building experiences.

An often overlooked aspect of outcomes is their relationship to higher values. While they may initially be utilitarian and solve immediate problems, they also need to resonate with your identity and values. When outcomes are meaningful, then you will be more motivated to achieve them. They need to support your higher purpose in leadership and in life.

There is a positive purpose to looking at the potential blocks to your outcome. Consider what stops you from having this outcome already. These blocks are issues that you will need to consider when working toward your goal. Whether it be lack of resources, inadequate authority, lack of skills, or opposition of others, these issues need to be considered and may require that you reformulate your outcome to deal with them. For example, you may have an outcome of sailing the length of the Mexican coast, but if you don't know how to sail a boat or don't even own a boat, you would need to deal with these issues first.

As a leader, specifying clear outcomes is critical to establishing the communication basis among your followers. When you state a well-formed outcome, those around you have a much better chance of determining if it is somewhere they want to go. Indeed, well-formed outcomes are the basis of follower alignment and motivation, as followers know exactly what it is that they are aligning with. Exercise 10.1 shows you how to develop well-formed outcomes that can align and motivate your followers.

Select an unresolved issue or situation that is important to you. Ask yourself each of the following questions in order and write down your answers. If an answer to a question causes you to reevaluate your answer to a previous question, go back and write down a new answer for that previous question and then continue answering the questions in order.

1. What do you want? What would you like to happen to resolve this issue? _

_____

_____

_____

_____

2. Is what you want stated in positive terms? *(For example: "I want X," not "I don't want Y.")* _____

_____

_____

_____

_____

(continued)

Exercise 10.1 Specifying a well-formed outcome.

(continued)

3. Is this outcome initiated and controlled by you? *(If it is not, then you run the risk of becoming stuck.)* _____

_____

_____

_____

4. What will you see, hear, feel, taste, and smell when you achieve the outcome? _____

_____

_____

_____

5. Is it an appropriate scope? Can you manage it easily, or is it more global in nature? _____

_____

_____

_____

6. What will having this outcome do for you? Will that be positive also?

_____

_____

_____

_____

7. What will be the evidence that you have achieved your outcome? _____

_____

_____

_____

_____

8. Where, when, and with whom do you want it? Where don't you want it, and where do you want it? _____

_____

_____

_____

_____

(continued)

Exercise 10.1   Specifying a well-formed outcome.

(continued)

9. How will having this outcome affect other parts of your life? What are the potential positive and negative consequences? _____

_____

_____

_____

_____

10. What prevents you from having this outcome already? _____

_____

_____

_____

11. What resources do you already have that will contribute to achieving your outcome? _____

_____

_____

_____

12. What additional resources do you need to achieve your outcome? _____

_____

_____

_____

_____

13. What path will you take to achieve your outcome? _____

_____

_____

_____

14. What are some alternative paths to achieve your outcome?

_____

_____

_____

_____

_____

Exercise 10.1 Specifying a well-formed outcome.

11

An Afternoon on the Bay

Michelle rocked back and forth in her porch chair, watching the branches of the large willow sway in the wind. It was early on a sunny Saturday morning, and it had been three days since she had spent time with Eric. Ever since she had eaten at La Fontaine it had all seemed to be a bit much—discovering her leadership metaphor, her values and beliefs, and how to clearly specify what she wanted. Her mind was swirling when she left the restaurant, and over these past three days she had gotten up early so that she could have some quiet time to sort things through.

Now her feelings of disorientation were fading, but she still felt angry and confused at how she was being treated at SpeedyCo. Thinking back on the last meeting with Tom and Steve, she recalled how frustrated she was when she left. Why had they been so patronizing? Even if his leadership metaphor was different from hers, Michelle thought that Tom shouldn't treat her with contempt and disdain or threaten her job. After all, she was trying as hard as she could—shouldn't she get some credit for that?

The ringing phone brought Michelle out of her reverie. It was Eric, suggesting that she and Randy meet him at the marina where he was taking his sailboat out on the bay.

"It is going to be a beautiful day, and wind and waves should be perfect for a sail," Eric said excitedly. "I've just finished refitting my new boat, and this will be her maiden voyage. Alexandra is home this weekend taking a break from her busy shooting schedule and will be along for the ride."

Michelle told Eric to hold on while she checked with Randy. Inside, she found him getting dressed for golf. When she asked him if he wanted to go sailing with Eric and Alexandra, he reminded her that he was playing several rounds of golf with his buddies and would be gone all day.

Michelle told him that she had some more questions for Eric and that she wanted to go sailing today. She felt she needed to sort some more things out with Eric's help. She told Randy that she really wanted to go with Eric and Alexandra. Randy replied that it would be okay and that he understood her wanting to be with Eric and Alexandra. Hugging him, she thanked him for understanding and walked back out onto the porch.

Eric exclaimed that it was great that she could make it and to pack extra clothes in case the waves came up and she got wet. Hanging up the phone, Michelle went into her bedroom and stuffed a change of clothes and a few personal items into a duffel bag.

While driving to the marina, Michelle thought about what a good friend Eric was and how she always felt glad to be around him. He seemed to have such a positive outlook on life and was always ready with a kind word or two. She remembered that he had once told her that he had been through a tremendous amount of personal growth and leadership training. She certainly could feel the results when they were together, as he always showed tremendous self-assuredness and confidence.

She rounded the corner into the marina, and before her were the masts of hundreds of sailboats bearing small, colorful flags that flapped in the breeze. After parking the car, she stepped out and immediately smelled the salt air and felt the warm bay breezes on her skin. Wavelets lapped against the hulls, of the boats, and sail lines pinged against the masts. Walking down the floating sidewalk past several large ocean-going boats, she saw Eric tending the sails on the deck of his boat, the Wind Dancer. Waving, she shouted out, "Hey, Eric, can I have permission to come aboard?"

Eric looked up and smiled. "Permission granted!"

The Wind Dancer was a 30-foot sailboat with a small cabin, a single mast, and brass and mahogany fittings. Her hull was a deep blue and showed the smooth lines of a sloop. There were three sails, the mainsail, the jib, and a rectangular spinnaker. The spinnaker more than doubled the mainsail area, and Eric used it when he really wanted to move across the water. The mainsail and jib were white, and the spinnaker was striped bright blue and red, which made quite a colorful sight when it was unfurled as the Wind Dancer sliced through the waves in the bay.

Michelle began helping Eric and Alexandra ready the boat for the day. After they had secured everything, Eric took the helm and started the engine, carefully piloting the boat out through the narrow channels of the marina. Once they were past the channel markers, Eric turned off the engine and began to unfurl the sails, motioning to Alexandra and Michelle to help him. They first raised the mainsail, and then the jib.

Suddenly, Michelle felt the boat shudder as the sails snapped out and caught the wind and the boat leaped across the waves as if pushed by a giant invisible hand. She grabbed a handrail as spray splashed across the deck. Eric said, "How are you doing?"

Michelle smiled and said, "Just great! This boat of yours is really amazing."

Eric nodded and said, "It took me a while to get the hang of sailing. I took a few months of lessons from a yacht club owner, and now I think I understand the basics. Every time I go out it is different—different wind, waves, currents. It's always a challenge and always fun."

Alexandra chimed in. "I just love sailing. I really like the feeling of being in alignment with the natural elements, and having the power of the wind take me where I want to go."

Michelle moved to the front of the boat and looked out over the bow. The sails were full and the water was clear and blue, sparking with a thousand points of sunlight. The ship moved easily across the waves, the sails billowing and the deck leaning to one side as Eric steered toward open water in the center of the bay. Michelle felt the sting of the salt spray on her cheeks and heard the gulls cry as they circled the boat.

After sailing for about an hour, they steered into a quiet cove next to a small island. Eric decided that this would be a good place to take a break, and Alexandra and Michelle lowered the sails and set the anchor. Eric went below, then emerged with three tall glasses of iced green tea. Michelle unfolded three deck chairs, and they all sat on the aft section looking out over the cove and the south end of the island. The palm trees swayed in the soft, warm breezes.

Michelle said, "This is so relaxing. I have been really uptight about SpeedyCo lately, and have been feeling angry and frustrated. This boat trip is just what I need—I feel really alive!"

Eric smiled and said, "It's good that you are aware of your feelings. What else are you feeling around SpeedyCo and your experience there?"

"I'm feeling enthusiastic about getting this customer service project done and hopeful that we will finish on schedule. However, I am also feeling threatened by Tom and Steve and their insistence on getting things done quickly. I'm feeling uncomfortable about the approaching deadline and nervous about getting the project completed."

Eric replied, "It sounds like you are afraid that you won't be able to complete the project, and that you are afraid that Tom and Steve might fire you if you can't do it as you had originally promised."

Michelle looked down and said, "That's right, I guess I am afraid yet at the same time I am passionate about the promise of my job and leading the project."

"It sounds like you are practicing the first part of emotional intelligence—being aware of your feelings."

Alexandra said, "Emotions are central to my work. As an actress I need to be able to strongly evince an emotion so that the audience feels exactly what my character is feeling at that moment. It took me a long time to become aware of just what emotion I wanted to put across, and I am still learning something new every day."

Michelle asked, "What is emotional intelligence exactly? I have heard a lot about it, but I'm not sure what it is."

"Emotional intelligence is an art, really. You need to identify your feelings when they occur, and then, by understanding your operating metaphor and values and beliefs, understand what need they are indicating either has or has not been met. Once you are aware of this need, you are able to choose your response, rather than just react on an emotional level. Emotional intelligence is a way of interacting compassionately with others while selecting your behaviors so that they support your outcomes."

"So you are saying that my underlying needs are driving my emotions?" she asked.

"Yes. Your underlying needs, beyond the physical needs for shelter, food, and rest, are really expressions of your values, which as you know stem from your operating metaphor in any particular context. Your values are intimately related to your identity and are what give your life meaning. They are the positive intentions around which you construct your life."

Michelle asked, "So how do I make sense of how I am feeling at SpeedyCo?"

Eric replied, "Well, the first thing to do is to be aware of what you are feeling. Then, determine the origin of the emotion—a need that was either being met or not being met. Finally, ask for an action that will result in your need being met. I know it sounds complicated, and you will get the hang of it with a little practice."

"I don't know, it sounds very complex and hard, and I really don't understand what I am supposed to do."

"Emotional intelligence is very much like being the captain of a sailboat," Eric said. "The world around you is in constant motion—the wind, the sun, the current, the waves, and the tides. The basic idea behind sailing a boat is to keep it in resonance with its environment—adapted to the changing conditions, using the energies present in wind and water to get somewhere. The opposite would be fighting the energies, being dissonant, and that will get you nowhere except perhaps sunk or stranded.

"So it is within you," he said. "Emotional intelligence allows you to be aware of the changing conditions within you and to steer yourself in the right direction. Just as on a perfect day like today with a fair wind and a following sea, the boat flows effortlessly through the water. When you practice emotional intelligence you move effortlessly through your world. Instead of fighting the energies that move and swirl through your world, you make choices based on your desired outcome and use the energies to propel you forward.

"Your values are like the structure of the boat—the size of the sails, the cut of the hull, the size of the keel. Different people with different types of values move through the world differently, taking different actions based on what's important to them and the changes that are happening around them. The key is to get your inner states resonating positively with your environment, just as when I have the sails perfectly trimmed and the wind and current are just right. It is not a static position, though, and it takes constant adjusting to stay on your path."

"As you saw when we were sailing today," he said, "I am constantly adjusting the sails and rudder to change direction with the wind and water, all the while keeping the destination in mind. The two keys for you to achieve emotional intelligence are awareness and self-management, knowing what is going on and managing it to get your desired outcome. The bottom line is if your values are being met or not. If they are not, you will be in a "negative' or downward emotional state; if they are, you will be in an 'expansive' or upward state."

Michelle leaned back in her chair and said, "I think I understand more what you mean now. I need to keep on top of my feelings—managing my reactions instead of engaging in emotional exchanges, especially when I get into it with Tom and Steve. I can think of a few heated conversations with them—maybe that's why things aren't going so well now."

Eric smiled and said, "You are right, I can remember a couple of times that you told me about that must have been very intense. It doesn't serve anyone to let things degenerate to that point, as you are merely expressing emotional energies instead of moving toward a resolution that benefits everyone."

The conversation fell quiet, and they listened to the waves lapping against the hull. The boat rocked gently back and forth, and the sun sparkled on the clear aqua water. Michelle breathed the salt air deeply and thought to herself that she would handle things differently in her life—she would be the captain of her own inner ship!

Michelle relaxed in her chair and sipped her tea. As the afternoon wore on Eric and Alexandra went swimming in the cove. She watched as they splashed about and snorkeled in the blue water. After a while, the quiet of the cove and gentle rocking of the boat lulled her into a peaceful slumber.

12

Alignment:
Resonating with Your Truth

UNDERSTANDING EMOTIONAL INTELLIGENCE

Emotions and the science of managing them have become more and more understood as social scientists have researched this topic over the past 25 years. An important result of this research has been an understanding of what skills comprise emotional intelligence and why it is a critical success factor for today's leaders. Studies conducted at Harvard University have shown that emotional intelligence is a primary factor for determining leadership success.

Emotions influence our thoughts and actions at a basic level, yet they often seem to defy logic and they aren't always easy to identify, understand, or explain. When you are happy, for example, you might be feeling excited, amused, proud, or exhilarated. When you feel a loss of confidence, you may also experience fear, nervousness, or misery—any of which can cause anxiety.

According to Daniel Goleman, in top leadership positions 80 percent of the difference of top performance is due to emotional competence. In a national insurance company, insurance agents who were weak in emotional intelligence sold policies with an average premium of $54,000. Those who were strong in key emotional intelligence capabilities sold policies worth an average $144,000. So we can see some real difference in those leaders with key emotional intelligence capabilities.

It is not accidental that certain emotional capabilities are found repeatedly in high performing leaders. Many of these emotional intelligence capabilities are demonstrated by leaders at all levels of organizations, from customer service representatives to CEOs. These capabilities have been shown to be distinguishing—that is, they are responsible for the high performance levels of outstanding leaders. So what is emotional intelligence, exactly?

We can define emotional intelligence as the capability to effectively manage yourself and your relationships with others. The purpose of developing emotional intelligence is to expand the ability to choose to be happy in all situations, regardless of your context. It is the ability to choose to make lemonade when life hands us lemons, rather than remaining stuck in bitterness and despair. It is knowing how to separate healthy from unhealthy feelings and how to turn negative feelings into positive ones.

Emotions are both indicators of our inner states and energizers of our external actions. As such, they contain powerful energies that we can wisely use to guide our lives and reach higher levels of fulfillment and happiness. If you ignore them or manage them carelessly, they have the power to destroy us and our relationships, sending us spinning down into a spiral of darkness. However, when we become skilled at sensing, labeling, and using our own emotions, we are able to harness them as a source of information and motivation. Emotions are the fuel for change—the challenge is to redirect and use that energy—to carefully choose how we will use the power of our feelings.

People are often told to control their emotions, to suppress anger, joy, or fear and cut them off from the decision-making process. This old way of thinking suggests that emotions make us less effective; however, nothing could be further from current research. Feelings provide insight, energy, and often are the real foundation for almost every decision. Instead of disconnecting our emotions, we need to create an opening in which we make the most creative, insightful, and powerful decisions. Particularly when dealing with conflict or crisis, we benefit by applying emotional intelligence skills, carefully engaging both heart and mind while creating productive solutions.

From the viewpoint of the inner leader, emotional intelligence is composed of three basic capabilities: the ability to be emotionally aware and fluent in discussing emotions; the ability to choose actions based on a neutral position rather than an emotional reaction; and the ability to bring authenticity to your life and live out your values. Choosing actions and living authentically can be considered emotional self-management skills. All three of these core capabilities can be learned and practiced until each is executed seamlessly, as part of your natural learned response. The end result is congruence and alignment of your inner selves—your identities, your values and beliefs, and your capabilities.

THE EMOTIONAL INTELLIGENCE PROCESS

We begin developing emotional intelligence with awareness. Awareness is composed of several smaller steps. First, you need to feel your feeling.

Notice the sensation in your body and your body's reaction to it. Where is it? In the pit of your stomach or the back of your neck?

The next step in emotional awareness is to acknowledge the feeling. This can be difficult, especially with negative feelings such as dread, fright, or misery. Many people may try to stop themselves from acknowledging their negative emotions by using drugs, alcohol, entertainment, or other distractions. They may also try to deny the existence of their negative feelings. Even education, memorization, intellectual, or religious pursuits can stop us from acknowledging our feelings. All of this defeats nature's purpose in supplying us with feelings.

As indicators of your inner state, your feelings are the basis of a very sophisticated guidance system. For this inner guidance system to function you must next acknowledge your feelings. Your negative feelings, for example, call your attention to things that are not healthy for you and let you know when you are out of balance. If you feel lonely, for example, you may need more connection with other people.

Once you have acknowledged your feelings, the next step is to specifically identify and label them. The more specific you are in identifying your feelings, the more accurate you can be in recognizing the unmet need and taking appropriate action. It also helps to identify the more primary feelings, such as anger, fear, and sadness.

The more you practice identifying emotions, the better you get at selecting the correct name for the feeling. Each time you identify an emotion and assign a label to it, the brain's cognitive and emotional systems work together to remember the emotion, the circumstances, and the label for the emotion. What you are actually doing is linking your cognition and emotion to create a new awareness that can be used to guide you to new choices for increased happiness.

By thinking about and identifying your feelings, you are taking the next step toward greater awareness. When your thoughts are clear and you understand your emotional states, you also feel more in control and empowered. You are building an understanding of what types of emotions appear in your body and a direct experience of the interaction of your thoughts, feelings, and actions. The goal of emotional awareness is to be fully literate in describing emotions as they arise so that you can gain a better understanding of their origin. The more that you observe your emotions and name them, the better you become at immediately identifying them and becoming comfortable with their existence.

Next, it is important to reflect on your feelings. As you practice emotional awareness, reflection will happen more and more quickly until it seems to occur in real time. Reflection is about observing the emotion and noticing it in your body as well as what label you have given it. By reflecting on emotions, you are building the foundation for choosing actions that best meet your needs. You then are better able to sort out all of those feelings, name them, and understand their causes and effects. By applying conscious reflection to your emotions, you come to understand their nature and watch them arise and subside, much like watching waves on a beach.

Another aspect of reflection is identifying the value or belief that generated the emotion. Knowing the aspect of your filter that caused you to feel a certain way is essential to living a life of integrity. Emotions, in this context, can be seen as indicators that tell you whether or not your values are being met in your current situation. A preponderance of contractive emotions tells you that something in your world is not aligned with what you really want and who you hold yourself to be.

Finally, after you have become aware of, acknowledged, identified, and reflected on your feelings, the last step in the emotional intelligence process is fully conscious choice. The first steps give you the space to choose what to do, rather than merely behaving based on reaction. Now you take advantage of that space and make conscious choice part of your strategy of living—it becomes a way of life rather than something to just think about. Conscious choice is also the basis of living in integrity—where your thoughts and actions align with your values, beliefs, and identity. You do what is right for you, always and with deliberate action.

You may be thinking that you are already making conscious choices in your life. This may be true to a degree. What the emotional intelligence process does is to allow you to be more fully aware of the driving force behind your choices so that you can decide if the direction in which these forces are sending you is where you really want to go. You realize a new perspective on the origin of your feelings, which enables you to expand the arena in which you make choices.

The emotional intelligence process is summarized graphically in Figure 12.1. When you contrast Figure 12.1 with Figure 3.2, we can see that the two steps summarizing the emotional intelligence process have been added More important, the main difference between Figure 3.2 and Figure 12.1 is one of reaction versus choice. Figure 3.2 shows a situation in which a person's behavior is in reaction to external stimuli passed through his or her map. He or she is reacting to circumstances based on his or her programming. When living life this way, it is easy for him or her to confuse the cause of their actions and difficult to discern what is really appropriate behavior. It is living with a short-circuited consciousness.

In Figure 12.1, however, we see the emotional intelligence process at work. Here there is integration of consciousness into the turbulent and sometimes confusing world of emotions. We have completed the circuit properly and added the additional processing power of our conscious minds to our emotional reality. We have become truly human, and we are using our

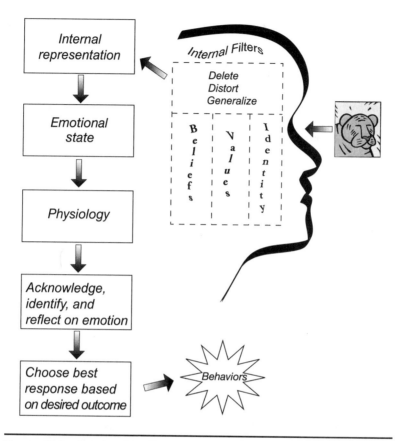

Figure 12.1   Emotional intelligence process.

native intelligence to guide ourselves down the path of congruency with our deepest-held values. We are living authentic lives.

There are numerous benefits to practicing emotional intelligence. The primary benefit comes in the form of flexibility. An important benefit is derived from Ashby's 1956 cybernetic principle of requisite variety: the element in a system with the most flexibility will be the controlling element. According to Glanville, "This law requires that a controlling system must have at least as much variety as the system it is to control. Control, as used here, indicates the ability of one system to direct another in the performance of the wishes of the first. Control is understood to exist when the behavior of one system is determined by another."

Translated into human terms, this means that the person with the greatest number of behavioral choices available will most effectively lead an organization. The more options a leader has to choose from, the greater the likelihood is that they will make a better decision. In order to effectively exert influence over a complex human system such as a modern-day business organization, a leader must be capable of choosing from a wide variety of behaviors. Rather than being "held hostage" by strong emotions, strong leaders move beyond reaction into self-awareness and self-management, choosing behaviors that are most appropriate based on their desired outcomes.

Emotional intelligence, from a process perspective, consists of two basic components: emotional awareness and emotional self-management. You must first become aware of your feelings—their intensity, location, depth, and flavor. After you have become adept at awareness and naming emotions, you can advance to the second component: managing your emotions to achieve optimal outcomes. You consciously choose your behaviors and responses based on your inner truth—your deepest values and needs. Awareness needs to be developed before you can practice self-management even though both are, once learned, practiced simultaneously. Eventually, practicing these components yields a life lived authentically and in integrity with your highest values.

LEADERSHIP LESSONS: DEVELOPING EMOTIONAL AWARENESS

Emotionally self-aware people set a strong foundation for making effective choices. They recognize how emotions affect their performance, both hindering and helping them as they pursue their desired goals. They are acutely aware of their own inner resources, abilities, and limits. This is especially valuable in high stress situations where team performance needs to be relied on for success. Interestingly enough, people who know their abilities and limits are also those who tend to use humor more often. Humor can be a critical factor in reducing stress in highly uncertain situations that demand top performance. Finally, emotionally self-aware people have a strong sense of self-confidence and a strong sense of their self-worth. These last qualities are especially important in establishing leadership presence and instilling a sense of trust in followers.

Emotions come in what we can call two basic flavors: expansive, or positive; and contractive, or negative. These are shown in Table 12.1 and Table 12.2. Expansive emotions occur when your needs are met, while contractive emotions occur when your needs are not being met. Expansive emotions increase your possibilities, while contractive emotions reduce your world to dismal sameness. Expansive emotions energize you for action, while contractive emotions reduce your will to act and hence your effectiveness and productivity. In either situation, you are experiencing an inner

Table 12.1   Expansive emotions.

Affectionate
- Compassionate
- Friendly
- Loving
- Open hearted
- Sympathetic
- Tender
- Warm

Confident
- Empowered
- Encouraged
- Open
- Optimistic
- Proud
- Safe
- Secure

Engaged
- Absorbed
- Alert
- Alive
- Concerned
- Curious
- Engrossed
- Enchanted
- Entranced
- Fascinated
- Interested
- Intrigued
- Involved
- Spellbound
- Pleasant
- Stimulated

Inspired
- Amazed
- Awed
- Wonder

Excited
- Adventurous
- Amazed

- Animated
- Ardent
- Aroused
- Astonished
- Dazzled
- Eager
- Energetic
- Enthusiastic
- Giddy
- Invigorated
- Keyed up
- Lively
- Passionate
- Perky
- Surprised
- Vibrant
- Zestful

Exhilarated
- Blissful
- Breathless
- Delighted
- Ecstatic
- Elated
- Enthralled
- Exuberant
- Radiant
- Rapturous
- Thrilled
- Upbeat
- Wide awake

Thankful
- Appreciative
- Moved
- Grateful
- Touched

Hopeful
- Expectant
- Encouraged

Joyful
- Amused
- Buoyant
- Cheerful
- Delighted
- Glad
- Gleeful
- Happy
- Jubilant
- Merry
- Pleased
- Mirthful
- Tickled

Peaceful
- Calm
- Clear headed
- Comfortable
- Centered
- Composed
- Content
- Cool
- Equanimous
- Fulfilled
- Mellow
- Quiet
- Relaxed
- Relieved
- Satisfied
- Serene
- Still
- Tranquil
- Trusting

Refreshed
- Enlivened
- Invigorated
- Rejuvenated
- Renewed
- Rested
- Restored
- Revived
- Splendid
- Wonderful

Table 12.2   Contractive emotions.

Afraid
- Apprehensive
- Dread
- Foreboding
- Frightened
- Horrified
- Mistrustful
- Panicked
- Petrified
- Scared
- Suspicious
- Terrified
- Wary
- Worried

Annoyed
- Aggravated
- Cross
- Dismayed
- Disgruntled
- Displeased
- Exasperated
- Frustrated
- Harried
- Impatient
- Irritated
- Irked

Angry
- Bitter
- Enraged
- Furious
- Hostile
- Incensed
- Indignant
- Irate
- Livid
- Mad
- Outraged
- Resentful

Aversion
- Animosity
- Appalled

- Contempt
- Disgusted
- Dislike
- Hate
- Hesitant
- Horrified
- Hostile
- Leery
- Repelled
- Repulsed

Confused
- Ambivalent
- Baffled
- Bewildered
- Conflicted
- Dazed
- Hesitant
- Indifferent
- Lost
- Mystified
- Overwhelmed
- Perplexed
- Puzzled
- Skeptical
- Torn
- Unglued
- Vexed

Disconnected
- Alienated
- Aloof
- Apathetic
- Bewildered
- Bored
- Cold
- Detached
- Disenchanted
- Distant
- Distracted
- Dull
- Indifferent
- Humdrum
- Lonely

- Numb
- Reluctant
- Removed
- Unconcerned
- Uninterested
- Withdrawn

Disquiet
- Agitated
- Alarmed
- Discombobulated
- Disconcerted
- Disturbed
- Guilty
- Perturbed
- Rattled
- Restless
- Sensitive
- Shocked
- Startled
- Surprised
- Troubled
- Turbulent
- Turmoil
- Uncomfortable
- Uneasy
- Unnerved
- Unsettled
- Unsteady
- Upset
- Worried

Embarrassed
- Ashamed
- Chagrined
- Flustered
- Guilty
- Mortified
- Self-conscious

Tired
- Beat
- Burnt out
- Depleted

(continued)

(continued)

Table 12.2   Contractive emotions.

• Exhausted	• Brokenhearted	• Frazzled
• Fatigued	• Depressed	• Irritable
• Lazy	• Dejected	• Jittery
• Lethargic	• Despair	• Nervous
• Listless	• Despondent	• Overwhelmed
• Passive	• Disappointed	• Restless
• Sleepy	• Discouraged	• Startled
• Spiritless	• Disheartened	• Stressed out
• Tepid	• Downcast	• Uptight
• Tired	• Forlorn	
• Weary	• Gloomy	**Vulnerable**
• Worn out	• Heavy hearted	• Fragile
	• Hopeless	• Guarded
Pain	• Melancholy	• Helpless
• Agony	• Morose	• Insecure
• Anguished	• Mournful	• Leery
• Bereaved	• Pessimistic	• Reserved
• Devastated	• Sorrowful	• Sensitive
• Grief	• Unhappy	• Shaky
• Heartbroken	• Wistful	
• Hurt	• Wretched	**Yearning**
• Lonely		• Envious
• Miserable	**Tense**	• Jealous
• Regretful	• Anxious	• Longing
• Remorseful	• Cranky	• Nostalgic
	• Distressed	• Pining
Sad	• Distraught	• Wistful
• Blah	• Edgy	
• Blue	• Fidgety	

state that you generate as a result of an external event passing through your map of reality.

I am choosing the terms *expansive* and *contractive* to remove any connotation that negative emotions are something to be avoided. Emotions are just energies, and labeling them positive or negative, good or bad, diminishes their power and usefulness. All emotions are equally valid as indicators and energizers, and it is in your level of awareness and how you manage them that you find your power. To deny or repress certain emotions because you label them bad is akin to walking on one leg—a difficult balancing job indeed! Moreover, it is not possible for you to manage yourself into an expansive emotional register unless you are equally familiar with your contractive states.

The bottom line is this: in order to effectively manage your behaviors, you need to be able to identify what you are feeling as well as the circumstances around which you generated that feeling. The more accurately you feel, acknowledge, identify, and reflect on your emotions, the better your foundation for choice.

What you are actually doing is creating an opening in time for choice to occur. This opening is the key to effective self-management and positive relationships. Rather than reacting from an "uncontrolled" emotional energy, you are dissociating from the energy and allowing yourself a pause during which you choose the response that is aligned with what you want. It is a practice of remaining centered amongst the maelstrom of life.

Exercise 12.1 is the first step to becoming emotionally intelligent. In this exercise you will become aware of and identify your emotions over a period of time. This exercise will increase your emotional awareness and fluency in expressing what it is that you are actually feeling.

Over the next 10 days, at three times during the day (morning, afternoon, and evening) make a point of noticing any significant emotions you feel and what you were doing at that time. Keep the timing of your entries consistent; for example, record your emotions at 10:00 A.M., 2:00 P.M., and 8:00 P.M. each day.

Review Table 12.1 and Table 12.2 if you need a specific term to describe what you are feeling at these times. Seek to identify each emotion to yourself as clearly as possible. Most of us have fairly distinct patterns of emotion that we experience time and time again. Once your diary is complete you will look for patterns both contractive and expansive.

If there are patterns of contractive feelings, look at the situations that triggered them. Are there common assumptions linking the situations and the feelings? What values were or were not being honored? What specifically was happening that caused this reaction?

If there are patterns of expansive emotions, then think about the situations and events that trigger them—it is very useful to have a clear idea about when and where you feel good, whether it is seeing friends, spending time with your family, completing a difficult task at work, or even shopping. Again ask yourself the questions from above. Are there common assumptions linking the situations and the feelings? What values were or were not being honored? What specifically was happening that caused this reaction?

You'll find that any notes you keep are helpful during the next section, on self-management.

Exercise 12.1 Keeping an emotional diary.

Week 1 Emotional Diary					
	Day 1	Day 2	Day 3	Day 4	Day 5
Time					
Doing					
Feeling					
Time					
Doing					
Feeling					
Time					
Doing					
Feeling					

Week 2 Emotional Diary					
	Day 6	Day 7	Day 8	Day 9	Day 10
Time					
Doing					
Feeling					
Time					
Doing					
Feeling					
Time					
Doing					
Feeling					

Figure 12.2 Emotional diary.

LEADERSHIP LESSONS: PRACTICING EMOTIONAL SELF-MANAGEMENT

Now that you have completed your Emotional Diary and achieved a basic level of emotional literacy, you are ready to embark upon learning the next emotional intelligence skill: self-management. As previously stated, emotional self-management consists of choosing actions and living authentically. These two skills can change your life completely, not to mention have a profound impact upon your effectiveness as a leader.

The two fundamental components of emotional self-management are these relatively simple commands: know yourself and choose yourself. By examining your values, beliefs, and needs, as well as your leadership metaphor, you come to know your map of reality. By understanding the process of emotional self-management, you choose to show up in the world with integrity and congruence.

Knowing yourself involves deeply understanding what makes you think, feel, and act in certain ways. It involves understanding which parts of your reactions are habitual or unconscious and which parts are consciously chosen. You recognize the causes of your own feelings and reactions. By being honest with yourself about your map of reality, you come to accept your own qualities and strengths, your own experiences and emotions, and your own power. Finally, you come to recognize both your right to choose yourself as a free person and the responsibilities of that choice.

Choosing yourself involves a profound awareness of what is right for you. It is based on an increased awareness of your responses so that you see your effect on others. It involves living without fear, never doing less than what is right for you. You hold yourself to high standards, even in the face of seemingly overwhelming negativity or hopelessness. With practice, you bring to the forefront of your mind a "checklist" of what is most important and you use it to weigh your decisions and actions. You recognize that you have choice, that you can make a difference, that you are an important part of a living organization. You choose to act to express your highest self in the world.

According to Dr. Sandra Scott, most of us are worried about other people's reactions and our own vulnerability when we express emotion. Those emotions that people often find hardest to express are the ones they personally find least acceptable—anger, fear or even love, for example. Even though emotions can sometimes be painful or difficult to show, there are five main reasons why it is useful for leaders to express and manage them.

1. When not expressed or released, emotional energies build internal pressure. Revealing your emotions to the appropriate person—somebody who

will not abuse the situation or your trust—can release an enormous amount of pressure in the right context. It is important to know the appropriate context and to show your emotions in an appropriate way. Relieving the internal pressure allows you to use your logical mind more effectively and to be more productive at your leadership tasks, including relating to others in a neutral way. When you are anxious or stressed from the buildup of too much pressure, emotions can cloud your mind and cause you to lose focus on your followers and the relevant organizational issues.

2. By hiding your emotions you can give the impression that you don't care—this can be damaging in any leadership setting. As a leader, showing compassion and caring for others is fundamental to building trust. Followers look to you as someone they want to respect, and you need to create a foundation for that respect. Transparency, or emotional openness, allows others to see you as you are and reveals that you are human just like the rest of us. Using an appropriate method of expressing your emotions shows your followers that you are in control of yourself and therefore are much more likely to be in control of the situation at hand.

3. Unchecked displays of anger, such as banging your fist on the table or verbally abusing others, can have disastrous consequences. As a leader, such openly uncontrolled displays of emotion can result in your followers' viewing you as one who cannot be trusted, for who knows how you might react when told of bad news or other undesirable information. In the same way, revealing your feelings to a person who will abuse them and violate your trust is equally inappropriate.

4. Appropriate displays of emotion also underpin self-assertiveness, which can show followers that you have a clear grasp of what is needed to move the organization forward and that you are willing to take a stand to make it happen. Knowing how to effectively express your emotions makes it easier to take a stand based on what is important to you. It also increases other people's perceptions of you as an honest person who is in control of yourself and the situation and as someone who will do what is necessary to move forward.

5. If somebody has upset you, is making too many demands of you, or just plain isn't doing what is required, and you don't show your emotions, they are unlikely to change their behavior. A central task in aligning others is getting them to voluntarily change their behaviors to achieve your outcomes or goals. Unless you let them know what you need and how you are feeling, they will continue on their old path.

In most leadership situations what is desperately needed are new behaviors from everyone in order to achieve stretch goals. As a leader, you cannot expect others to change unless you share with them your emotional state and ask them to meet your needs—which, in some cases, include both your values as well as your leadership outcomes. Statements such as "I am feeling excited about this project and would really like to know that you are on board as a key player for our team" can create a space for followers to choose to align themselves with both your excitement and the project outcomes.

People who are good at emotional self-management exhibit self-control and keep disruptive emotions and impulses to a minimum, not permitting angry outbursts to destroy or damage relationships. They maintain integrity and act in congruence with their values. They are also adaptable to change, showing flexibility when dealing with difficult situations. They have initiative and are proactive in their lives, striving to reach a high standard of performance excellence. Finally, those who are adept at emotional self-management tend to be optimistic about the future. This is because they have shown resilience and persistence in pursuing goals despite obstacles and setbacks. They view a failure as just another learning experience.

The human brain follows patterns, or neural pathways. Stimulus leads to response and, over time, the response becomes habitual as it becomes ingrained in your subconscious mind. This is the basic path of all human learning. Once a habit has established itself at this subconscious level, however, extraordinary measures are required to change it.

Patterns in your life include thinking, feeling, and action in a continuous cycle. During childhood, you learn lessons of how to cope, how to get your needs met, and how to protect yourself. These strategies reinforce one another, and you developed a complex structure of identity, values, and beliefs to support the validity of the behaviors.

Often this system of patterns serves you well, and at other times it leads you to unconsciously create the opposite of what you really want. The key is to understand that all behaviors are appropriate in some context, and therefore it is imperative for you to make sure that your behaviors are appropriate for the context in which you find yourself. Avoiding unconscious sabotage is paramount to effective leadership.

How can you make sure your behavior is appropriate at both the conscious and unconscious levels? First, by becoming emotionally literate. Second, by practicing choice—choosing what you do based on what your desired outcome is in a particular situation. The goal here is to make choices that result in your maintaining a positive emotional register. The intensity of emotions, however, can often limit your choices as you struggle with powerful feelings.

The problem is that contractive emotional surges, by directing your blood flow away from your brain, can quite literally shut off your ability to think clearly. Such emotions are the body's way of making you pay attention to a perceived threat. When communicated outward, these emotions have the power to shut down the thinking processes of an entire group or organization, rendering you useless as a leader.

The importance of positive emotions cannot be overstressed. Because of a phenomenon known as limbic resonance, other people are able to understand your emotional states without any oral communication at all on your part. That means that you do not have to communicate orally, yet you still send a strong emotional message nonetheless. By staying in control of your emotions, you send a message of trust, comfort, and fairness.

When you communicate in a positive emotional tone, you give yourself and others permission to feel more creative and productive, and you foster the ability to think clearly. Positive emotions, unlike contractive emotions, can direct additional blood flow to your brain, enhancing your ability to think clearly. Gratitude, thankfulness, and laughter shut down your anger and shift you out of a contractive state.

Emotional self-management is based on using language to support what you really want to have happen in any situation. There are two ways to practice emotional self-management: communicating from needs and reframing the situation. Both of these methods shift you into a more positive emotional register, clearing your mind and giving you the space to choose more rationally.

Communicating from Needs

Communicating from needs forms the basis of a shared understanding among all humans. This is because basic human needs are universal and do not vary that much from culture to culture. According to Marshall Rosenberg, the basic human needs are the foundations of values and principles found the world over. These are shown in Table 12.3.

When you state what you want in terms of your basic needs, you enable others to see your motivation and the force behind your feelings. This immediately establishes the basis for rapport, as well as enabling you to better understand how your needs and values drive your emotions. The need-based communication process is as follows:

Observe your inner state

- You observe an external event that affects your well-being.

- You generate a feeling in relation to what you are observing.

- You observe and understand the nature and source of the feeling—the needs and values that created it.

Table 12.3 List of basic human needs.

Connection
- Acceptance
- Affection
- Appreciation
- Attention
- Be right
- Be liked
- Belonging
- Cooperation
- Communication
- Closeness
- Community
- Companionship
- Compassion
- Consideration
- Consistency
- Empathy
- Inclusion
- Intimacy
- Love
- Mutuality
- Needed
- Nurturing
- Praise
- Respect/Self-respect
- Safety
- Security
- Stability
- Support
- To know and be known
- To see and be seen
- To understand and be understood
- Trust
- Valued

- Warmth
- Worthwhile

Honesty
- Authenticity
- Integrity
- Presence

Play
- Joy
- Humor

Peace
- Balance
- Beauty
- Comfort
- Communion
- Ease
- Equality
- Harmony
- Inspiration
- Order

Physical health
- Air
- Food
- Movement/exercise
- Rest/sleep
- Sexual expression
- Safety
- Shelter
- Touch
- Water

Meaning
- Achievement
- Accuracy
- Adventure
- Awareness
- Celebration of life
- Challenge
- Clarity
- Competence
- Consciousness
- Contribution
- Control
- Creativity
- Discovery
- Effectiveness
- Growth
- Happiness
- Hope
- Learning
- Make a Difference
- Mourning
- Order
- Participation
- Purpose
- Risk
- Self-expression
- Stimulation
- To matter
- Understanding

Autonomy
- Choice
- Freedom
- Independence
- Space
- Spontaneity

Ask for what you need

- You describe your present observation—what you perceive is going on.

- You describe your feelings about what is going on.

- You describe the reason for the feeling—your need or value that is not being met.

- You request a concrete action that will meet your need in the situation and achieve your desired outcome—an action that will enable you to achieve a positive emotional register.

With practice, the first part of this process can take place in an instant. This part is simply the emotional awareness that you learned in the previous section. The second part, however, requires a bit more finesse, as you will need to think through what you really want to have happen in the situation. When expressing your desired action, you need to be aware of the consequences of what you want to happen—do they align with your desired outcomes in the situation?

When specifying the consequences, you need to explain any positive and negative consequences you foresee. These could also be expressed as potential costs and benefits for others when they give you what you want. From the opening you have created in yourself by using your emotional literacy, you are creating an opening for your followers to step through to follow your path and achieve your desired outcome. You are inviting them to follow you in full knowledge of the potential advantages and drawbacks of your proposed path and goals. Not only are you choosing for yourself, but you also are allowing others to choose for themselves. This is a deceptively simple yet incredibly powerful leadership skill.

For example, Chandra was part of a training class in which everyone was required to contribute their experiences and ideas for a class project. One person in the class, Linda, did not participate. When asked to participate, Linda said, "I have nothing to add" and "I don't want to." The group moved on and continued to hear from the other members.

Chandra saw Linda respond like this twice, and after the second time became very angry about Linda's lack of participation. Chandra was swept up in a wave of strong emotion, and she struggled to control herself. After some consideration, Chandra made the following statement to Linda:

> Linda, each of us, including me, paid a lot of money to take this seminar. We all agreed to play by the rules of the game as part of taking the class. Now I see you not playing by the rules and not participating, yet you still want to be in the class. I am feeling angry and irritated at your behavior. I am also feeling disrespected.

I need to feel respect from those I associate with, you in this case. I ask that you either play by the rules and participate fully, or leave the class. If you participate you get to help us create our project and be part of the team. If you leave then you will miss a valuable learning experience.

Interestingly enough, Chandra went on to understand that Linda was not disrespecting her, but that she was insecure and afraid to participate. Linda went on to participate fully and became one of the most creative members of the class. Linda became more secure in knowing that it was safe to express herself and that others in the class wanted her to participate fully. She ended up astounding the other students with her enthusiasm and creative energy.

By stating your story, your feelings, and your needs and by asking that your needs be met, you are behaving authentically. You are living in accord with your values, which comprise the essence of your character—you are in integrity with yourself. In leadership, integrity is an essential characteristic. Without it, you cannot ask others to follow you. With it, you will be perceived as forthright and honest, and others will be more inclined to follow you readily.

Exercise 12.2 allows you to practice communicating from needs. Perform this exercise at first alone, and then practice out loud with a group to become familiar with the mechanics of it. In time the four steps will flow effortlessly.

Reframing

Reframing is a powerful technique that can completely shift your perspective on a given situation. It means to put a new or different perspective around an image or experience. From a psychological perspective, reframing changes the meaning of something by placing it in a different framework or context. A frame determines how an event or experience is interpreted and what your internal representation is, thus generating specific emotions. When you can change your interpretation, you can shift your emotional state at will into a positive register, opening yourself up for making more choices.

There are two types of reframing techniques: content and context. Each is useful in its own right, and when skillfully practiced each can quickly shift your emotional state into the positive register.

Context reframing has to do with shifting the context of an event, that is, the circumstances in which it takes place. Think of context reframing as shifting the physical location of an event to change its meaning. Content reframing, on the other hand, has to do with changing our perspective of a particular event—looking at it from a different viewpoint as a result of gaining other

Step 1: Describe your present observations. What is your story about what is going on? Who or what do you want to blame or credit for the situation? _____

Step 2: Describe what you are feeling (refer to Table 12.1 on page 97 and Table 12.2 on pages 98–99). Be honest and clear. Where in your body are you experiencing these emotions? Get in touch with the feeling. Is more than one feeling present? _____

Step 3: Explain the reason for your feeling. What value or need is not being met? What value or need is being met? What do you really need that you didn't get? What are you afraid of losing? What did you expect to have happen? _____

Step 4: Make a choice and ask for what you want. What do you want to have happen? How can your need or value be met? How can you feel more positive? What outcome do you want? Once you have decided this, communicate it to the other person. _____

Exercise 12.2   Communicating from needs.

information. It is interpreting an event differently as a result of new or additional information.

A content reframe example in the world of human behavior might be John, who is always negative at meetings, often criticizing ideas offered and looking at the downside of proposals. He seems to poke holes in whatever anyone suggests and finds reasons why proposed actions will not work. Rather than condemn such behavior or put John down as a person ("That John, he's always so negative!"), we can reframe his behavior. We could look at it from the viewpoint of his providing a more realistic appraisal of situations and alerting the group to potential downfalls or weaknesses. His comments can be used to strengthen proposals and ideas by pointing out areas that need to be addressed prior to implementation.

Content reframing looks at the positive intent behind a behavior as well as at the positive benefits a behavior could serve in relation to a larger system or bigger "picture" of what is going on. Positive intent is what NLP presupposes is behind every behavior, and that our conditioning or mental maps cause us to exhibit less than optimal behaviors. A common content reframe during any conflict is to realize that people have preferences for different representational systems (visual, auditory, or kinesthetic). This allows you to view other persons with a new level of awareness and to realize that they have not necessarily been acting out of hate or anger, but rather because they sense the world in a different manner, represent their experiences differently, and thus behave in a different way.

Common content reframing questions are the following:

- What is the positive intention behind this behavior?

- What possible positive outcomes could this behavior achieve?

- How does this behavior fit into the bigger picture of what is going on?

Context reframing in the world of behavior can help you appreciate that every behavior is useful in some context. It leads you to refocus on issues related to the larger context or to see how a behavior might be useful in a different setting. For example, Fred, who is outgoing and aggressive, is causing some resentment among his peers in the Engineering Department. As a director, you reframe this type of behavior and see that it would be very helpful in a Technical Sales position. This might lead you to offer him the

---

- Be specific about what you are feeling—don't exaggerate.
- Be specific about the circumstances in which you experienced the emotion.
- Be clear about your needs and values that you feel were not met.
- Take responsibility for your emotions and your happiness.
- Examine your own feelings rather than the actions or motives of other people.
- Develop constructive coping skills for specific moods. Learn to relax when your emotions are running high and to get up and move when you are feeling down.
- Look for humor or a life lesson in a negative situation.
- Be honest with yourself. Acknowledge your feelings, look for their source, and come up with a way to solve the underlying problem.
- Realize that emotional self-management will take time and patience.

Figure 12.3 Tips for emotional self-management.

position, explaining how it would enable him to be more outgoing and actively pursue clients. A common context reframe question is to ask, "Where might this behavior be useful in my organization?"

As you practice communicating from needs and reframing the situations around you, there are some general guidelines that will help you to remain focused. These guidelines are shown in Figure 12.3.

13

An Evening on the Island

Michelle awoke to the sound of Eric digging around in the ship's cabin. She turned and noticed Alexandra assembling some things on the deck. Alexandra smiled and said, "You have been asleep for quite a while now. I hope you had a good nap!"

The sun had gone down considerably, and the afternoon had gotten on quite a bit. Some high clouds had gathered and were drifting toward them. Eric popped his head up above the deck and said, "Get your things—you are in for a surprise!" Alexandra smiled mysteriously and said, "I wish Randy was here to share this."

Michelle felt excited and a bit confused—what did Eric have in mind? She went below and gathered her things into a waterproof duffel bag Eric had placed on the bunk. She emerged from the cabin asking, "So what is up now?"

Eric smiled and said, "I am going to show you something special. Follow me!" With that, he took his bag and climbed over the side of the boat into a small raft bobbing in the warm, aqua water. Alexandra and Michelle followed him into the raft, and taking up the oars, paddled toward shore.

As the shoreline got closer, Michelle could see an opening in the bushes next to a small palm grove. "Steer for the opening there," Eric said. They paddled vigorously and splashed their way through the small waves onto the shore. They beached the raft and dragged it into a clearing to the side of the palm grove, where Eric tied it to a tree.

Michelle followed Eric and Alexandra as they walked down the path, following the base of a small cliff through the dense subtropical forest. After walking for 20 minutes, they came upon another clearing, this time with a small house in the center of it. Eric walked up to the door, took out a key, and unlocked the door with a smile. "Eric, is this your house?" Michelle asked incredulously.

"Yes, it was nothing more than a dream many years ago. After deciding that I really wanted this place, I came to realize how important being here was for me. So I was really motivated to build it. I call it Satori. Can you spend the night here with us tonight?"

Alexandra chimed in: "I come here to recharge during breaks in my hectic movie schedules. It offers me a peace and quiet that I haven't found anywhere else. I always leave feeling refreshed. Sometimes I get up early and go for a swim in the ocean, just me, the waves, the sand, sun and the birds. It is a great place for renewal."

Michelle told them that she needed to check with Randy. After a brief call on her cell phone, she told the pair that she would be more than happy to spend the night.

"Great! I'll get the guest room ready." said Alexandra. "Come with me and you can put your things in there."

They walked through the living room and kitchen to two small bed-rooms at the rear of the house. Alexandra motioned to the room on the right, and Michelle strode in and placed her duffle on a low dresser. She noticed the rice paper windows between the rooms as well as the futon beds that were little more than platforms. There were two small white lamps on a table next to the head of the bed.

Going back into the kitchen where Eric was making green tea, she asked, "What does the word *Satori* mean? This place has a very oriental feel to it—does that have anything to do with the name?"

"Yes, the name is a Zen word. It means enlightenment characterized by a sudden, all-encompassing vision or complete understanding, as a result of a breakthrough from meditation. Satori lies beyond discrimination and dif-ferentiation, and it is considered part of Zen training. I thought of it when I was taking martial arts some years ago."

Michelle asked, "But why did you decide to build this house here on the island? You could have just bought a condo or vacation time share somewhere."

"Several years ago, right after I met Alexandra, we discussed the value of meditation and having a space in which we could practice quietly, some-where away from it all yet close to the bay and the ocean. The layout of this place is designed to support my martial arts and our meditation practice, which are really important to us. I have always thought of myself as a seeker who finds new ideas and brings them to the world. Thus having a place where I could seek, if you will, was very important. Also, during this time it was very stressful for me at Boil Industries, where I worked before coming to Floriant. I needed a quiet place to use as a retreat."

"How was it possible for you to build this place? Wasn't it really expensive?"

"Actually, after I had decided that this was what I really wanted to do, things just sort of fell into place. I felt so strongly about having this place and living in it that I never questioned it would happen. I visited a friend's home that he built on an island similar to this one, and we talked about how he had done it—his trials and tribulations, how difficult it was for him to get the building materials to the island, how the contractors didn't follow the plans, and other things like that. I knew that it was possible to build this place—my friend had done a very similar thing."

Michelle asked, "How did you know what to do or even where to start? It seems like such a complicated endeavor. There is so much to organize and with all of the rules about building on this island, you probably had to navigate a maze of regulations."

"My friend gave me a lot of tips about using local building materials and contractors, altering the design to lower construction costs and take advantage of some climate-based efficiency measures. I seemed to find the money as I needed it through loans and savings. So everything came together the way I had envisioned."

"Where did you learn about building a home? After all, your formal schooling was in psychology and management. It seems like you would have to learn a lot just to figure out where to start."

Eric laughed and said, "I took at class in home construction at Copeland Community College. It covered everything and the instructor was great. He and I even met several times after the class was over to discuss the project, and we have become friends over the years. He has even been here and stayed overnight several times. He said he was proud of what his star pupil had done."

Michelle smiled and said, "Eric, you always seem to know just how to go about things. This place is marvelous!"

"Yes, I really enjoy coming here on weekends and for vacation. You know, I think the toughest part of the whole project was believing in myself enough so that I could move forward. For years I had struggled with self-image, and as I practiced my martial arts, I dropped about 30 pounds and gained a tremendous amount of self-confidence. I also began to take full responsibility for my life and all that was happening in it, unlike I had done in the past. After this major shift, everything else just seemed to come naturally."

Alexandra walked into the kitchen, and she and Eric began preparing the evening meal. Michelle went out onto the porch, letting the door close with a thump behind her. She reclined in a large wicker chair with over-stuffed white cushions, placing her green tea on the table next to her.

She looked out through a few bushes to the beach, where several small boats were drawn up under a palm tree and two girls played, laughing in the water. Above her, she could hear birds twittering, mingling with the sound of the waves from the sea. She smelled the lush sweetness of the flowers growing next to the house. The now-cool breeze from the ocean flowed across her skin, moving through the forest and gently swaying the branches of the palm trees above her.

Michelle felt very much at peace, and she took a deep breath as she leaned back in the chair. "What a great place" she thought. "Someday Randy and I will have a house like this."

14

Motivation: Energizing for Success

UNDERSTANDING MOTIVATION

One of the most important leadership skills is to be able to develop the energy to propel yourself toward an outcome of your own choosing without losing momentum along the way. To do this requires motivation—the sustained engagement of your internal desires.

The word *motivation* is derived from the Latin meaning "to move." In essence, you take action because it feels rewarding to do so. Your challenge is to manage and maintain your energy levels so you can persevere through the difficulties. To do this, you must tap into the "being" part of yourself and find the reward that you truly value. Otherwise, you are dependent on feedback from others and can easily be swayed from your true intentions. As you learn to get the validation you need from inside, you also create inner strength and the power to grow continually. This process is shown graphically in Figure 14.1.

Emotional intelligence, including the ability to exercise optimism, reinforces your long-term motivation because it allows you see the future as positive and worthwhile. Maintaining expansive emotions is the vehicle to propel you beyond the present and enthusiastically anticipate the future. Emotional intelligence is tied to resiliency and to perseverance, which are two skills that most affect your ability to function despite the stresses and challenges of day-to-day life. Optimism means recognizing that we each have the power to make change—that we make a difference—and that through our efforts the world can improve. Because your feelings toward the future are experienced in the present, positive thinking immediately enhances your life.

Supporting emotional intelligence is a series of beliefs that energize your actions and move you forward powerfully. These beliefs act together to create a resonant framework, quickly moving you down the path of your

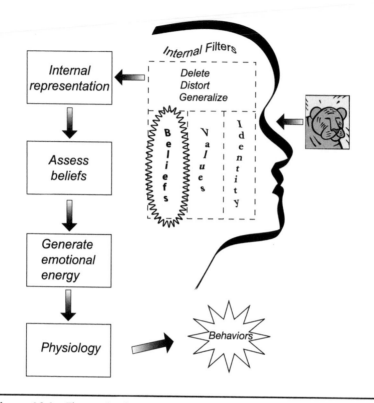

Figure 14.1   The motivation process.

true desires. They determine how much effort you will make and how long you will sustain it in the face of obstacles and challenges.

LEADERSHIP LESSONS: STRENGTHENING YOUR MOTIVATION

People look to you, as a leader, to exhibit enthusiasm and confidence about your stated outcomes. These energies are essential to bettering your chances for success. Since you are creating a space to attract people, you will need to fill it with passion and self-assurance. By examining your own beliefs related to your motivation, and by making sure they are in line with your map of reality, you are expressing yourself with integrity and transparency—you are then perceived as an authentic person. Your authenticity will resonate with your followers as you reinforce your optimistic outlook.

Assessing Belief 1: Desirability

The first belief to examine is the desirability of the goal. Is it worth it to you to go after this outcome? How does the outcome help you to express your identity in the world? How does the outcome support your values? Is it something really important to you?

Goals and outcomes that we strongly desire for ourselves are always important to us, sometimes for a variety of reasons. They are usually related to our metaphor of identity and values, and they are further heightened in importance by the events surrounding our lives. An important goal usually fills both immediate and long-term needs. Moreover, your goal and the current events of your life should reinforce each other. Current events can provide the extra drive for you to achieve important goals that resonate with your identity and values.

When you really want to achieve a goal and it is important to you, you need to focus also on what you stand to lose and what you stand to gain by achieving it. In order to make the effort, you need to see that the benefits of achievement will far outweigh the drawbacks of staying where you are now. If you find that the drawbacks of achievement are greater than the benefits, then you will have difficulty in getting yourself to be motivated to achieve the goal and you will need to find some further incentive.

Here is where you will need to revisit your leadership purpose and the measurements that you use to determine when you are achieving your purpose. Will achieving your goal result in more of those items that you use to measure the success of your leadership purpose (e.g., learning and knowledge, wealth, production, belonging and community, and photographs/stories), as shown in Figure 5.3 on page 45? If the answer to this question is yes, then this is a direct indication that your outcome is important to you at an identity level.

Assessing Belief 2: Possibility

The second belief that you should examine is the possibility of achieving the goal. Is this something that is far-fetched, or does it stand a reasonable chance of becoming a reality? Has anyone else done something similar? Can you clearly visualize it? Where else in the world has it been done?

However, just because something has not been done does not mean that you should not believe it to be possible. Indeed, many of the great inventions of our time were created by "dreamers" who believed in their visions and the possibility that they could turn them into reality. Just look at Walt Disney and what he succeeded in creating. Nothing like what he envisioned had ever existed, yet he persisted in his dream because he truly believed that it was possible. He created theme parks that today generate billions of dollars in revenue and create happiness for people of all ages throughout the world.

What you should seek is a balance of imagination, passion, and reality. While many things are possible, it may take more than one lifetime or more resources than you have available to achieve them. The key is to define what actions will most likely lead you to achieving this outcome and to know that they will be effective. If you do what you are proposing to do, you are certain you will reach your outcome. How do you know? From having performed similar actions, or having watched someone else perform similar actions, and observing the results. Once you understand what actions will be required and how they could be effective, your belief in the possibility of the outcome will be greatly strengthened.

Assessing Belief 3: Appropriateness

The third belief you should examine concerns the actual actions you plan on taking to achieve your outcome. Given your current situation and what you are planning on doing, are these actions appropriate? Will they result in your planned outcome? Are they realistic, or will taking these actions severely affect another area of your life? Are they so difficult that performing them raises a huge barrier?

When looking at the appropriateness of any actions, you should first ask yourself, "Are they the best way to go about achieving the outcome, or are there other ways to arrive at the same place? How will taking this action result in my desired outcome?" Make sure that your proposed actions are the best way to achieve your outcome.

For example, if your outcome is to be a doctor, then you will need to go through medical school. Going to airline mechanics school would not be appropriate! The action you need to take is clear and appropriate. Another example might be, "If I make more sales calls then I will make more sales." This appropriate action could be based on the times you were successful while on sales calls.

A second question to ask about this belief is whether the action fits with your current environment. Is it ecological? Will it cause problems in another part of your life? In the first example, you may need to go to medical school, but it may require a large financial commitment that conflicts with your family needs, or it may require that you leave your family and set out on your own with no support. In the second example, you may already be working 60 hours a week making sales calls and any additional time would be an unacceptable burden. In these cases the action may not be ecological. Your choice, however, still needs to be weighed against the importance of your goal to determine your overall motivation.

Assessing Belief 4: Capability

The fourth belief that you should evaluate is that you have the capabilities and skills to reach your outcome. It is your belief about your ability to perform a particular behavior successfully. In the example of medical school, you need to believe that you are capable of succeeding in school.

Also, even though you may not currently possess the skills, you still need to believe that you are capable of acquiring them. For example, if your action involves complex computer programming and you don't have the required skills or knowledge, but you know about a class where you can gain these skills, you will believe that you can acquire the skills necessary to perform your programming. The key is to know that you either have the skills or can get them in a reasonable way.

Assessing Belief 5: Self-Esteem

The fifth belief relates to your self-image and self-esteem. Basically, you must hold yourself as a worthy person deserving of the outcome. According to Tracy Turner, self-esteem "means that we appreciate ourselves and our personal worth. More specifically, it means . . .

- we have a positive attitude

- we evaluate ourselves highly

- we are convinced of our own abilities

- we see ourselves as competent . . . in control of our own lives and able to do what we want."

You must ask yourself, "Do I deserve this in my life?" Supporting your beliefs of deservedness are a well-understood identity, value system, and skill set. You have confidence in your abilities from the actions you have taken— you know what you have done and understand your impact on the world. When you know who you are, what is important and practice emotional intelligence, you can develop positive self-esteem and feelings of deservedness.

All five of these beliefs (shown in Figure 14.2) work together and create your level of motivation. The effect is multiplicative; that is, each magnifies the influence of the others to create an overall belief level. If one belief is not present, or is present to a lesser degree, your overall motivation level will decrease accordingly. This is why it is important to assess each belief, developing the ones that are lower or are not well-supported so that your overall motivation level is adequate for leading.

The second part of motivation is generating emotional energy and allowing its expansion to move you forward even faster. Once your supporting beliefs are in place, your emotions will resonate in the expansive register. To

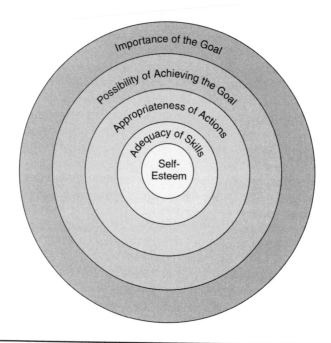

Figure 14.2 Components of personal motivation.

effectively arouse the same emotions in others, infuse your speech and actions with positive emotions. Express yourself emotionally as you perform the tasks that move you to your desired goals. Embrace your positive emotions and feel them fully in your body. Rejoice in knowing that your outcome is becoming real, that you are taking positive steps in a direction of your own choosing, and that you are using your skills to bring you what you want in your world. You are gaining strength and achieving mastery.

Before embarking on a project, it is important for you to assess your motivation so that others will perceive you as having the required energy levels to which they are attracted. You then need to work on any beliefs that may be limiting you from having the motivation you desire. You may want to look at related beliefs, reference experiences, support from peers and colleagues, and process tools to bring each belief into a completely positive and fully developed state. Once you have done so, you can be assured that your motivation to achieve the outcome will be as high as possible.

Human motivation can be compared with a hot air balloon, as in Figure 14.3. When the balloon is deflated, it sits on the ground and goes nowhere. Thus it is when our motivation is low—we stay in one spot and do nothing about the issue. We are a crumpled mess on the ground!

When all of our motivational beliefs are present, however, we have a large balloon ready to rise. When one or more beliefs are missing, our balloon

Figure 14.3 Our motivation helps us soar.

is much smaller. With a small balloon, no matter how much energy you put into inflating it, it just might not be big enough to lift you off the ground! This is why it is important to assess and develop each of your motivational beliefs. You want to have the biggest possible balloon!

Once you have created the balloon, you still need to get it off the ground. Much like turning on the burner in a hot-air balloon, when we generate emotional energy our beliefs inflate and lift us, and off we go. Just as a hot-air balloon expands with air and rises, when we are motivated our spirits lift and we move toward what we want—we are no longer stuck. We rise above obstacles and soar to our intended destination. We have a wider view and expand our horizons of what is possible for us. Our positive beliefs give us the potential to rise, and our emotional energy fills our balloon with hope and optimism.

Exercise 14.1 provides a series of questions to assess your motivational beliefs. You are guided through a set of detailed questions that allow you to determine beliefs that may be limiting your motivation, and you are encouraged to seek answers that can increase the power of these beliefs. Exercise 14.2 provides steps to increase the emotional energy around your beliefs, thus increasing your motivation.

Step 1: Define your outcome. Write out a brief description of the outcome.

_____

_____

_____

Step 2: Write out a brief description of your plan or solution to reach this outcome._____

_____

_____

Step 3: Is this outcome important to you? Is it worth the effort to attain the outcome? _____

This outcome is important because _____

_____

_____

It is worth the effort to attain this outcome because _____

_____

_____

Step 4: Is it possible to achieve this outcome? _____

_____

_____

It is possible to achieve this outcome because _____

_____

_____

Step 5: Is what has to be done to achieve this outcome understood and appropriate? _____

_____

_____

I understand what has to be done as follows: _____

_____

What has to be done is appropriate because _____

_____

_____

(continued)

Exercise 14.1   Assessing your motivational beliefs.

(continued)

Step 6: Do I have the skills and capabilities to achieve the outcome?

I have the skills and capabilities to achieve the outcome because _

_____

_____

Step 7: Am I deserving and responsible to achieve this outcome? _____

_____

_____

I deserve to achieve this outcome because _____

_____

_____

I am responsible for achieving this outcome because _____

_____

_____

_____

Step 8: Evaluate your responses for Steps 3 through 7. Determine those of greatest concern, that is, those that are weakest.

_____

_____

_____

Step 9: Look for related experiences, support from peers and colleagues, alternate scenarios, process tools, or related beliefs to strengthen this belief. What can you change to increase the strength of this belief? _____

_____

_____

_____

Step 10: Repeat Step 9 for each belief until you reach your highest possible level of belief._____

_____

_____

_____

Exercise 14.1   Assessing your motivational beliefs.

In this exercise you focus on your outcome and generate positive emotional energy. Find a place where you will not be disturbed for at least 15 minutes. Close your eyes, relax, and breathe deeply.

1. Imagine yourself having your desired outcome already. Picture it in your mind's eye.

2. Really enjoy the outcome and bring it into a clearer reality. Embrace it with all your senses—what do you see, hear, and do while you are enjoying the outcome?

3. Feel your feelings in your body. Where are they located? How intense are they? What is their quality—smooth, electric, or flowing?

4. Now we will adjust the sensory qualities of your internal representation of the outcome.

   • Move the image around in a way that feels more motivating or compelling. Adjust the color, brightness, saturation, hue, distance, and size.

   • Add or change the sounds associated with the outcome. Adjust their loudness, tonal quality, and rate so that they are more pleasing.

   • Add or change the activities you are doing while enjoying the outcome. Change the rate of your movements, making them quicker or slower. Adjust how many things you are doing, adding to or subtracting from the number of activities. Make your movements either mechanical or flowing. Which combination feels best?

5. Once you have adjusted the visual, auditory, and kinesthetic components of your internal representation, fully experience the expansive feelings that come from achieving this outcome. Feel these great feelings in your body. Locate them and describe them to yourself—their location, intensity, and quality.

6. Now picture yourself doing the things that move you toward your outcome. Remember the expansive feelings as you see yourself performing the activities.

7. Now open your eyes and bring the visualization to a close.

8. Each time you go about an activity that will achieve your outcome in the real world, remember the feelings you generated during this exercise.

Exercise 14.2   Generating emotional energy.

15

Sunrise at Satori

Michelle opened her eyes and looked over at the clock. The pale blue numbers read 5:30 A.M. She quietly dressed, pulling her windbreaker over her head and slipping on a pair of sandals. Walking past the other bedroom, she could hear Eric and Alexandra breathing steadily.

Opening the front door and walking through the palm grove, she looked up at the palm trees and into the pale blue sky beyond. She strode forth onto the beach and sat down about 15 feet from where the water reached. The waves, now wavelets of foam, had calmed down as the tide had gone out. From the trees came the first few chirps of the awakening birds. She breathed the cool salt air in and felt deeply invigorated. The first pink ribbons of dawn were spreading across the sky, and the morning star shone clear and bright.

Last night her dreams had been jumbled, but this morning she awoke with a new clarity. She knew exactly what she would do at SpeedyCo. First, she would blend her leadership metaphor with Tom's so that they could both get what they wanted. She would emphasize her values of rules and boundaries, casting them in a new light so that Tom could see how they clearly supported his desire to play a winning game. She would stress developing a winning team that used the rules to their advantage. She would show how the training would make everyone a better player and would enable them to build on their natural ability to win.

Also, she was going to rewrite her project plan to make sure all of its outcomes and goals were clearly and positively specified. She was going to call a project team meeting first thing Monday morning to get everyone involved. She would use the instructions that Eric had given her to restate her goals and outcomes for the entire customer satisfaction project.

She also realized that she needed to become better at managing her emotions. Even if Tom and Steve had strong personalities, she felt that she could improve her responses and interactions with them by carefully managing her feelings and responses. She remembered a few times when she had given up after feeling overwhelmed, and she vowed that this would not happen again. The first chance for her to practice would be at the meeting where she was going to roll out the revised customer satisfaction project plan.

She understood why her job was important to her, what she needed to do to make things better, and she shouldered her leadership responsibilities squarely. She knew that she had the skills to achieve her goals and that it was possible for her to do so. A new resolve arose in her, stirring strong feelings of confidence and passion. She would make it happen.

She stood and walked into the shallow water. The waves gently washed over her feet as she raised her eyes to the dawning of a new day.

16

Soaring to Success

" "Tom, if you take a quick look at these numbers you'll see what I mean," Michelle stated strongly. "From the standpoint of effectiveness, we are looking at what I think is the fastest way to keep us even with the other major players out there. These systems, once the organization has really learned them, should enable us to rally the team around our customer needs and expectations."

Michelle had been preparing this presentation for Tom and Steve over the past three days. During that time she had met with each of the department managers responsible for implementing different pieces of the customer service initiative—information technology, technical writing, human resources, and facilities and operations. She had revisited her project plan and made sure each of the goals and milestones was clearly specified and within the authority of the managers.

Tom stated rather dryly, "Haven't we been over all this before? I think it may be time to look at skipping this training program."

Steve chimed in, "We keep our customers satisfied and our salespeople are trained to do a good job at this. What do we need this type of training for anyway?"

Michelle felt herself flush with anger. How could they be saying this? After all the time she spent on the proposal. Thinking through her emotion, she realized that it was her values of respect and professionalism that weren't being met. She also realized that she could reframe the situation by looking at it from a different viewpoint—by seeing Tom and Steve as being too preoccupied with their jobs to have time to understand the details of her plan.

She spoke steadily and clearly. "Tom and Steve, I have been over this program with you four times. Each time you have rejected it out of hand. I feel very frustrated and disheartened by your comments. It is important for me to get the respect of my coworkers and be treated as a professional. I ask that you take a time out and listen carefully to my plan for this training. I have reviewed this with all the other department managers, and they concur with its structure and milestones. I would ask that you give this training one more chance to be put into play."

Tom twisted uncomfortably in his chair. "We have been tough on you about this training. The board of directors is really pushing me this quarter to show some improvements in profits, so I am taking a look at everything we invest in very carefully."

Steve began, "Yes, we've got to make sure everything helps us to be a winner and doesn't . . ." Tom held up his hand and gestured stiffly for Steve to stop.

"Look, Michelle—I'm under a lot of pressure from the board, so give me something I can take to them," Tom said. "Tell me how this initiative will improve our bottom line."

Michelle took a deep breath and recalled the outcome she wanted from this meeting. She wanted Tom and Steve to approve the budget and plan for the implementation of the customer service initiative in its entirety. She also wanted them to acknowledge her as a professional and realize the amount of work that she had put into planning the activities. She also realized that she needed to motivate Tom by showing how the initiative met his need for profits and that the company's capabilities were sufficient to implement it successfully.

"Tom, customer service needs to be an essential element of our competitive strategy. Achieving strong profitability and market share requires loyal customers—those that will stay with us and make positive referrals. Our goal in this customer service initiative is to build loyalty into our customer base. Loyal customers will place a priority on doing business with us and will pay a premium for our products and services. We get about 65 percent of our business from existing customers. Since it costs five times more to find a new customer than to keep an existing one happy, it is much more profitable for us to build satisfaction and loyalty into our customer base than to focus on getting new customers.

"Our game plan is to get all the players that deal with customers up to speed as quickly as possible," she said. "You can see how we are using a phased approach to implementing the systems."

Tom glanced down at the budget and project plan and nodded his head. Steve was looking at the task listings as Michelle continued.

"We are going to center on what it takes to win the game—getting and keeping customers. We are going to understand their needs and expectations. Part of the play will be to listen to them and link what they tell us back to the bench—the R&D, design and manufacturing people. We are also going to concentrate on helping the star players on Steve's sales force do what they do best. We'll do this by building a complaint-handling system. That will free them to play their finest game, and to develop positive relationships with each customer. The rest of the team will evaluate and improve our processes for getting our customers what they want and building their loyalty."

Michelle continued to explain how the customer service initiative would benefit SpeedyCo financially, and she showed Tom and Steve the phased approach that minimized the amount of time each employee would spend in training while dispersing key knowledge throughout the organization. She emphasized how the team could still keep in the game while changing its strategy and tactics. Explaining how the company as a whole would benefit from the training, Michelle shows how improved customer service would generate a 150 percent return on the system's implementation investment.

She went into a task by task review of what she had planned to have happen. Tom's face began to soften as he realized that Michelle had thought through this plan completely, and it wouldn't hinder operations, as he had feared.

After reviewing the tasks, Michelle glanced over at Steve, who smiled and said, "I can really see how this will let my most valuable players do what they do best and will support them in building a strong customer base. I think these systems will really help us to be much more competitive—we'll be better prepared to make the big plays with some of our larger customers."

"So where do we go next with this, Michelle?" Tom asked.

"After you approve the budget, I'll begin implementing the training and get the IT folks busy deploying the supporting technology. The rest will unfold as stated here in the plan."

"How long will it be until we can realize some revenue gains on this?"

"Well, with the new product roll-out next quarter, our profit margins will increase as the newer units replace the old ones," she said. "By keeping our current customers satisfied and loyal, I'm estimating a positive return from increased sales within the next three quarters. I intend to coach all the managers through this so it will go smoothly and to make sure everyone is ready to play a bigger game."

Turning in his chair, Tom said, "Well, what do you think, Steve?"

"Michelle has certainly thought this thing through. I can use all the help my team members can get. I can see how this new customer information and complaint handling will really boost our performance. We will be free us to focus on closing bigger sales with our established accounts. I am ready to give it a shot and see how we handle it."

"Steve, remember, we are going to do some training for your team, too" Michelle said. "I'll be there to coach your guys through this so they can quickly come up to speed with the latest systems and stay out on the field making sales. We are going to minimize the bench time for everyone."

Tom, flourishing his pen, quickly signed the letter Michelle had prepared. "Michelle, this is a go. Let's move out on this and get rolling. I am going to make a presentation about this at the next board meeting. I'll use what you have given me here and will let you know if I need more figures. In the meantime I suggest you contact your direct reports and let them know the next six months are going to be extremely busy for them!"

Michelle beamed and said, "Thanks, Tom. I'll start on this today and get everyone moving. This is an incredible new strategy, one I know can bring us some big wins."

Michelle left Tom's office and walked down the hall to her office, thinking that the tough work had really just started, not only for her project but for her as a leader. She had used the coaching Eric had given her to achieve her outcome at this meeting. She knew, however, that there would be many such meetings in the coming months. It would take focus and determination to carry out her leadership role and to stay her planned course.

She committed herself to develop her leadership skills as the initiative progressed. She would do whatever it took to be a successful leader. She knew that it would take time to develop her skills and that flawlessly executing her leadership role would not happen overnight. Still, she knew she could do it—she would do it. Today she had shown herself what she was capable of, and she vowed that she would not let herself or her team down. She would find the leader in herself.

Glossary

Alignment—The degree of congruence among one's internal logical levels, that is, environment, behaviors, capabilities, values, and identity. A person is in alignment when all of his or her logical levels are in appropriate relation with one another.

Effectiveness—The quality of achieving an intended goal or outcome. Effective people are able to achieve their designated goals.

Efficiency—Skillfulness in avoiding wasted effort. It involves using only the minimum resources necessary to achieve a designated purpose.

Integrity—The degree of congruence among one's behaviors, values, and identity. It involves living in a state of authenticity, humility, and grace, guided by the awareness of change, impermanence, and the immediacy of death.

Leadership—Influencing others to achieve a particular set of outcomes. It requires the demonstrated ability to provide guidance and direction, based on the use of skills and capabilities that direct the operations and performance of others.

Metaphor—A figure of speech in which an expression is used to refer to something that it does not literally denote in order to suggest a similarity. It promotes understanding one thing in terms of another. Examples include "I have butterflies in my stomach," "ship of state," "drowning in money," and "you are the sunshine of my life."

Neuro-Linguistic Programming (NLP)—The study of the structure of subjective experience. NLP focuses on the interactions among the brain (neuro), language (linguistic) and the body (programming). It includes technologies and methodologies for applying a comprehensive system of knowledge and values. NLP, which emphasizes the transfer and practical application of skills in different contexts, is based on modeling states of excellence.

Neurological levels—A natural hierarchy of information classification that describes the types of neurological processing required to interpret and comprehend specific types of knowledge derived from study, experience, or instruction. Higher-level processing mobilizes and extensively engages the nervous system, while lower-level processing involves passive adjustment of primary sense organs. A sense of self arises from total mobilization of the nervous system at all other levels.

Operating metaphor—A metaphor used in a particular context, such as leading, parenting, being a friend, or managing an organization. An operating metaphor is specific to a context, and it may overlap or coincide with a person's life metaphor. It may be thought of as part of the mask of identity used when performing a specific role.

Values—A set of ideals accepted or prized by an individual or group. Values are also principles in which a person or group is emotionally invested (either for or against something).

Sources and References

Allen, James. *As a Man Thinketh*. New York: Peter Pauper Press, 1973.

Covey, Steven. *The 7 Habits of Highly Effective People*. Salt Lake City: Franklin-Covey Company, 1998.

Dewey, Barbara. *As You Believe*. Fort Wayne, IN: Knoll Publishing, 1990.

Dilts, Robert. *Visionary Leadership Skills*. Capitola, CA: Meta Publications, 1996.

Dilts, Robert, and Judith Delozier. *Encyclopedia of Systemic NLP and NLP Coding*. Scotts Valley, CA: NLP University Press, 2000.

Dilts, Robert, and Robert McDonald. *Tools of the Spirit*. Capitola, CA: Meta Publications, 1997.

Faulkner, Charles. *Creating Irresistible Influence with NLP*. Niles, IL: Nightingale-Conant, 2002.

Faulkner, Charles. *How Do We Know What to Want?* http://www.achieveingexcellence.com, 2004.

Frankl, Victor. *Man's Search for Meaning*. Boston: Beacon Press, 1959.

Glanville, Ranulph. *The Value of Being Unmanageable: Variety and Creativity in CyberSpace,* in: Proceedings of the Conference "Global Village '97," Vienna. 1997.

Goleman, Daniel, et al. *Primal Leadership*. Cambridge, MA: Harvard Business School Press, 2002.

Gordon, Judith. *A Diagnostic Approach to Organizational Behavior*. Newton, MA: Allyn & Bacon, 1987.

Hesselbein, Frances, and Paul M. Cohen, eds. *Leader to Leader*. Jossey-Bass, 1999.

Huber, Cheri. *Projection Teleclass*. Murphys, CA: Zen Monastery Practice Center, 2004.

Kotter, John. What Leaders Really Do." *Harvard Business Review,* December 2001.

Lakoff, George, and Mark Johnson. *Metaphors We Live By*. Chicago: University of Chicago Press, 2003.

Lynn, Adele B. *Applying Emotional Intelligence at Work*. Belle Vernon, PA: Bajon House Publishing, 2001.

Mitsch, Darelyn, ed. *Coaching for Extraordinary Results*. Alexandria, VA: ASTD, 2002.

Morgan, Gareth. *Images of Organization: The Executive Edition.* San Francisco: Berrett-Koehler Publishers, 1998.

NLP Comprehensive. *NLP Practitioner Training Participant Notes,* NLP Comprehensive, 2003.

Peltier, Bruce. *The Psychology of Executive Coaching.* New York: Brunner-Routledge, 2001.

Reynolds, Marcia. *Accessing Emotional Intelligence.* Phoenix: Covisioning, 2003.

Rosenberg, Marshall B. *Non-Violent Communication: A Language of Life.* Encinitas, CA: PuddleDancer Press, 2003.

Scott, Sandra. *Get Confident.* BBC Health, 2004.

Turner, Tracy. *Self-Esteem.* BBC Health, 2004.

Whitworth, Laura, Henry Kimsey-House, and Phil Sandahl. *Co-Active Coaching.* Palo Alto, CA: Davies-Black Publishing, 1998.

Zimmer, Heinrich. *Philosophies of India.* Princeton, NJ: Princeton University Press, 1951.

Index

A

alignment
  defined, 135
  internal alignment, 7, 72
  of others, 103–4
  of people, 70, 72, 82
anger, 103
authenticity, 6, 24, 64, 72, 92, 95, 102, 118
awareness, 6, 92–93, 96
awareness levels, 17–19

B

Bandler, Richard, 13
behaviors, 17–18
  management of, 100
beliefs and values, 17–19, 35, 37, 61.
    See also values and beliefs
  limiting vs. fostering beliefs, 61–62
body language, 104

C

Capabilities, 17–19, 37
cognitive processes, 13
commitment, 72
communication, 14, 71
  language and NLP, 14
  need-based process, 105–6, 109–11
  reframing and, 108–10
congruency, 70–72
content reframing, 108–10

context reframing, 108–10
contractive (negative) emotions, 96, 98–99
control, 91, 95
core values, 5. *See also* values and beliefs
Creating Irresistible Influence with NLP (Faulkner), 44

D

Dilts, Robert, 13
Disney, Walt, 119
distortion, 16–17, 81

E

effectiveness, defined, 135
efficiency, defined, 135
emotional awareness, 92–93, 96
  developing of, 96–101
emotional diary, 100
emotional intelligence, 70
  authenticity and, 92
  basic capabilities of, 92
  basic components of, 96
  choice based on neutral position, 92
  as conscious process, 94
  defined, 92
  emotional awareness and fluency, 92, 96
  emotional self-management, 71, 96
  graphical representation of, 95

long-term motivation and, 117
  practicing of, 95
  process of, 92–96
  reaction vs. choice, 94, 96
  understanding of, 91–92
emotional openness, 103
emotional self-management, 71, 96
  choosing yourself, 102
  communicating from needs, 105–8
  expressing emotion, 102–3
  knowing yourself, 102
  patterns of, 104
  practicing of, 102–11
  reframing, 108–10
  self-control, 104
  tips for, 111
emotional state, 15, 18
  internal, 21
emotions
  contractive (negative), 96, 98–99
  expansive (positive), 96–97, 99
  expressing and managing of,
    102–3
  identification of, 93
  positive emotions, 104
  reflections on, 93–94
  values/beliefs generating, 94
environment level, 7–10
expansive (positive) emotions, 96–97,
  99

F

Faulkner, Charles, 37, 44
focus concept, 80
fostering beliefs, 61–62

G

generalization, 17, 81
Glanville, R., 95
goals, 119. *See also* outcomes
Goleman, Daniel, 91
Grinder, John, 13

H

herd conditioning, 5
Huber, Cheri, 39

human behavior, 13
human needs, 107–8
humor, 96

I

identity, 4–5, 17–19, 36
  fulfillment of, 35
  leadership and, 37
  metaphors of, 35–42
information, 13, 44
  internal filters of, 16–17
  neurological levels of experience
    and, 18–20
information overload, 16
inner leadership
  key tasks of, 7, 21
integrity, 6, 94, 104, 108
  defined, 135
intellectual capabilities, 18–19
internal alignment, 72
internal emotional state, 21

K

Kant, Immanuel, 15
Kotter, John, 70

L

leadership
  awareness and, 6
  the being of, 6–7, 22–24, 69
  defined, 135
  the doing of, 7, 22–24, 69–73
  elements for success, 71
  emotional intelligence and, 91
  inner alignment for success, 7, 72
  key to effectiveness, 5
  leaders as "attractors," 72
  mental maps, 21, 59
  projection/outpicturing of identity,
    23, 39
  role assignment/function and, 23,
    44–45
  three primary activities of, 70
  visualizing outcomes, 79
  wants, definition of, 80–84
leadership metaphor, 35, 37–38, 69

common themes and effects of, 38, 40–42
defining of, 47, 49–51
example of, 47–48
projection and, 39
roles within themes, 44
self-discovery of, 43
values as perceptual filter, 60
leadership purpose, 43–44, 69
examples of, 46
statement of purpose, 46
life metaphor, 37–38
limbic resonance, 104
limiting beliefs, 61–62
loyalty, 23, 72

M

mental capabilities, 18–19
mental maps, 21, 59
metaphor. *See also* leadership metaphor
defined, 37, 135
life metaphors, 37–48
operating metaphor, 59, 136
motivation, 17, 35
appropriateness of actions, 120
capabilities and skills, 121
components of personal motivation, 122
defined, 117
desirability of goal, 119
graphical representation of, 118
of people, 70, 72, 82
personal beliefs assessment, 124–25
possibility of achievement, 119–20
self-esteem and, 121–23
strengthening of, 118–25
understanding of, 117–18

N

need-based communication process, 105–6
needs
asking for what is needed, 107
basic human needs, 106–7
communicating from, 105–8
observing inner state, 105
negative emotions, 96, 98–99

negativity trap, 81
Neuro-Linguistic Programming (NLP), 6
cognitive processes and, 13
defined, 13, 135
graphical representation of, 14
internal map of reality, 15, 17
linguistic component of, 14
mental maps and, 21
as modeling technology, 14
perceptual differences and, 13
positive intent and, 110
programming component of, 14
neurological levels, 18–20, 35
defined, 136

O

operating metaphor
defined, 136
values and beliefs and, 58
optimism, 117
organizational culture, 23
organizational reward system, 39
outcomes. *See also* motivation
choosing behaviors for, 96
higher values and, 81–82
importance of, 79
personal responsibility for, 80
positive/negative consequences of, 107
specifying well-formed outcomes, 82–84

P

perceptual filters/differences, 13, 60
perseverance, 117
personal awareness, 6, 92–93, 96
personal motivation. *See* motivation
personal responsibility, 80
positive emotions, 96–97, 99, 104, 117
precision concept, 80
professionalism, 61
projection, 39

R

reaction vs. choice, 94
reflection, 93

reframing, 108–10
    content and, 108–10
    context and, 108–10
renewal value, 61
resiliency, 117
reward system, 39
Roberts, Monty, 71–72
role assignment/function, 23, 44–45
Rosenberg, Marshall, 105

S

Satori, 114
Scott, Sandra, 102
self-assertiveness, 103
self-awareness. *See* emotional awareness
self-confidence, 96
self-control, 104
self-discovery, 4–5
self-esteem, 96, 121–23
self-image, 121–23
self-knowledge, 6, 73, 80
self-management, 100–1. *See also*
    emotional self-management
self-motivation, 70
sensory inputs, 16–17
skills, 19
SpeedyCo case study
    background information, 9–11
    core values and beliefs, 53–58

emotional intelligence and values,
    85–89
goal specification and outcomes,
    75–78
implementation and action plan,
    127–32
motivation for success, 113–16
nesting/aligning metaphor of
    identity, 31–33
strategy, setting direction and, 70

T

teams, 70
thinking process, 15–17
transparency, 103
trust, 60, 71, 96

V

value attribution, 35
values and beliefs, 17–19, 35, 37, 69, 108
    articulation of, 63–65
    examples of, 64
    limiting/fostering beliefs, 61–62
    list of, 62
    operating metaphor and, 58, 136
    as perceptual filters, 60
vision, 79–80